11·09·09

THE DERBYSHIRE TIMES
RAILWAY ALBUM

Compiled by Clive Hardy

www.derbyshiretimes.co.uk

Derbyshire TIMES

at heart ♡ publications

First published in 2008 by
At Heart Ltd
32 Stamford Street
Altrincham
Cheshire
WA14 1EY

in conjunction with
Derbyshire Times
37 Station Road
Chesterfield
S41 7XD

ISBN: 978-1-84547-200-9

Printed and bound by Ashford Colour Press, Gosport.

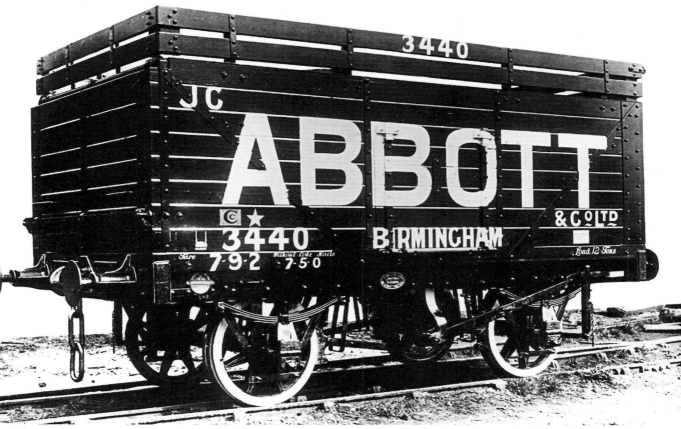

One of the many wagons built by the Derbyshire Carriage & Wagon Co, New Whittington, Chesterfield. (Chesterfield Local Studies Library)

INTRODUCTION

Welcome to the Derbyshire Times Railway Album; a collection of newspaper, library and readers' photographs that take a look at the railways past and present within our circulation area. This is not a full blown railway history book; it is primarily a collection of pictures, though we hope there will be things in here to interest the general reader and railway enthusiast alike. Images date from the late nineteenth century to 2008 and have been arranged as far as possible in route order so pictures of the Cromford & High Peak line begin at Cromford and go by way of Sheep Pasture, Middleton Top, Friden, Parsley Hay to Ladmanlow and then to Buxton. Similarly pictures of the old Midland main line from Derby to Manchester begin at Matlock Bath and continue to Chinley via Matlock, Darley Dale, Rowsley, Bakewell, Hassop, Millers Dale, Great Rocks Junction and Peak Forest.

There are one or two places where it was impossible to carry on the flow. From Chinley there is a detour to the Dinting Railway Centre and the Derbyshire section of the Woodhead route, prior to us heading off along the Hope Valley line, through Chesterfield and on to Hasland and the remnants of the narrow gauge Ashover Light Railway. We then have a selection of pictures covering the former Great Central, Lancashire, Derbyshire & East Coast, and Midland lines to the east of Chesterfield, including Barrow Hill, Staveley Works, Langwith Junction and so on. We then head off along the Cromford & High Peak line to Buxton before finishing with pictures taken at Wirksworth and the Midland Railway Centre at Butterley.

For the non-railway reader, here are a few terms to help you with the captions. Steam locomotives are often referred to by the name of the chief mechanical engineer (CME) responsible for their overall design; followed by their class or power classification and their wheel arrangement.

In the picture on the following page, the passenger train is being hauled by a Stanier Black Five 4-6-0. In other words the engine was designed by the LMS Chief Mechanical Engineer, William Stanier. The 'Black' simply refers to the lined black livery worn by this class; and the 'Five' is its power classification. The 4-6-0 is the wheel arrangement of the locomotive, not including its tender; so it has a leading two-axle bogie (four wheels) and three coupled axles (six wheels), the middle one taking the drive from the cylinders. The zero simply means there are no supporting wheels under the firebox or cab. To the right is a Fowler 0-6-0 4F. In other words, it was designed by Henry Fowler; the 0-6-0 means it has only three axles, the wheels on each side being linked together with a coupling rod. The 4F is its power classification as a freight engine, so a Stanier 8F would be a locomotive designed by William Stanier that was twice as powerful as the Fowler machine. A 0-6-0T has its water in two

BR liveried Stanier Black Five 4-6-0 No.44817 hurtles past LMS liveried Fowler 4F No.3991 at Tapton near Chesterfield. (C.M & J.M.Bentley)

tanks, one either side of the boiler. A 0-6-0ST has its water in a tank that drapes over the top of the boiler – a bit like a saddle over the back of a horse.

With diesels, Co-Co simply means that the locomotive has two three-axle bogies and all axles are powered, whereas 1Co-Co1 means the locomotive has an unpowered leading axle on each of its bogies.

Railwaymen often refer to trains travelling in either direction as 'Up' or a 'Down'. This has nothing to do with geography. Historically, trains always travelled 'Up' to the most important town on a route, so a train going from Derby to London would be in the 'Up' direction, while a train from London to Derby would be in the 'Down' direction.

Beyond that the essential aim of this book is to entertain, so sit back, browse and enjoy it.

Clive Hardy
May 2008

THE OLD MIDLAND MAIN LINE AND PEAK RAIL

A south-bound train rattles through Matlock Bath in this picture which was originally published as a postcard. In the distance what appears to be a north-bound stopping service picks up speed as it heads towards Matlock itself. The station building, with its distinctive Alpine look, still stands, though the goods shed and goods yard have long since been consigned to history and the land they once occupied is now a car park.

Riber Castle Wildlife Park near Matlock dates from the 1860s and is well-known for its fauna reserve. There was a time, however, when it was also home to a couple of steam locomotives; one a 9.5inch gauge Battison 4-6-2 *Lady Joyce;* the other this 0-4-0ST built by Peckett & Son of Bristol in 1920. Our picture was taken on 7 July 1971 when the Peckett had just arrived at Riber. It hadn't come far – just up the hill from the nearby Cawdor Limestone Quarries owned by Derbyshire Limestone. Looking on is owner Peter Bell and his 18-month-old son Marcus.

Matlock is now the northern terminus of the former Midland Railway main line to Manchester and here on Friday 15 February 2008, a two-car Class158 diesel multiple unit forms the 11.12hrs departure for Derby. The picture was taken from the disused platform 2 which Peak Rail wish to reactivate in the not-too-distant future to create interchange facilities for passengers.

The 158 still sports its Central Trains livery and though the company still existed as a legal entity, at the time it was in the process of winding up its affairs as it had lost the franchise. Central Trains began operations on 2 March 1997 after National Express won the franchise to take over what had been BR's Regional Railways sector operating over 1,758 route miles of the network.

Operating a weekday schedule of over 1,300 services, and responsible for 87 staffed and 106 unstaffed stations, Central was awarded a subsidy of £187.5 million in its first year, though this had fallen to £132.6 million in 2003/4.

The Central Trains/Midland Mainline, which was at least breaking even, Silverlink County and Virgin Cross Country franchises were amalgamated and then split into three new ones; East Midlands, West Midlands and New Cross Country.

Matlock station on 15 February 2008. The last steam-hauled passenger train to run through Matlock was 1Z70 on 10 June 1968, hauled by BR Britannia Class7 4-6-2 No.70013 *Oliver Cromwell.*

Stanier Jubilee 4-6-0 No.5654 *Hood* pulls out of Matlock at the head of a north-bound train on 20 July 1946.

TRAVEL BY TRAIN TO BAKEWELL SHOW

THURSDAY, 4th AUGUST
NEW AND IMPROVED TRAIN SERVICES

Outward Departure Times.

From		a.m.	a.m.	a.m.	a.m.	a.m.	a.m.	a.m.	a.m.	p.m.	p.m.	p.m.	p.m.	p.m.	p.m.	p.m.	p.m.
Whatstandwell	dep.	—	—	10.52	—	—	—	—	—	—	—	—	—	—	—	1.32	1.57
Cromford	,,	—	—	10.59	—	—	—	—	—	—	—	—	—	—	—	1.39	2.4
Matlock Bath	,,	—	—	11.3	—	—	—	—	—	12.9	12.37	12.44	—	—	—	1.43	2.8
Matlock	,,	10.2	10.12	10.37	11.8	11.17	11.49	11.26	12.4	12.14	12.41	12.48	1.0	1.29	1.47	2.13
Darley Dale	,,	—	—	10.43	11.14	11.23	—	—	—	—	—	—	—	—	1.53	2.19
Rowsley	,,	—	—	11.20	—	—	—	—	—	—	—	—	—	2.0	2.25
Bakewell	arr.	10.16	10.26	10.55	11.28	11.35	12.4	11.45	12.18	12.42	12.56	1.4	1.14	1.42	2.8	2.32

SPECIAL CHEAP RETURN FARES (THIRD CLASS).

Whatstandwell	2/8	Matlock	1/6
Cromford	2/2	Darley Dale	1/1
Matlock Bath	1/8	Rowsley	10d.

AVAILABLE OUTWARD AND RETURN BY ANY TRAIN ON DAY OF ISSUE.

RETURN SERVICES FROM BAKEWELL.
To Matlock, Belper and Derby — 4.35 p.m., 5.43 p.m., 6.3 p.m., 7.45 p.m., 8.5 p.m.
To Matlock and Matlock Bath — 7.13 p.m., 7.30 p.m., 8.15 p.m.
To Darley Dale and Matlock — 7.20 p.m.
To all Stations — 4.47 p.m., 6.13 p.m., 8.25 p.m., 9.2 p.m.

SPECIAL CHEAP SINGLE TICKETS (THIRD CLASS).
AVAILABLE BY ALL RETURN SERVICES
From BAKEWELL to

Rowsley	5.	Matlock Bath	1/2
Darley Dale	10d.	Cromford	1/5
Matlock	1/1	Whatstandwell	1/9

BRITISH RAILWAYS

On a visit from the East Somerset Railway, artist David Shepherd's BR Standard Class 9F 2-10-0 No.92203 *Black Prince* stands at Darley Dale with a Peak Rail train for Matlock Riverside.

Though designed to work heavy mineral traffic, the 9F's top speed of 90mph also saw them putting in appearances hauling summer passenger trains. Following successful trials in March 1960, four 9Fs No's.92203–92206 were allocated the Bath Green Park to work holiday services to Bournemouth. March 1960 was also the month when the last of the class and the last steam locomotive to be built for BR, No.92220 *Evening Star*, was completed at Swindon Works. (Baz Blood)

This well-known picture taken by Harry Townley on 8 August 1953 shows the original Rowsley station of 1849, which was designed by Joseph Paxton for the Manchester, Buxton, Matlock & Midland Junction Railway. For 11 years Rowsley was the northern terminus of this grandly-titled railway, but during 1860 work began on extending the railway – now a part of the Midland – towards Buxton via Bakewell. However, the extension northwards was made on a new alignment just over a quarter of a mile south of this station, effectively leaving Rowsley marooned at the end of a spur. With the opening of Bakewell and Hassop stations Rowsley closed to passengers, though it remained open for goods traffic. (C.M. & J.M.Bentley)

Designed by Manchester-based architect Edward Walters, the second Rowsley station was built by John Wood of Derby as part of a three station contract that also included Bakewell and Hassop stations. The Midland Railway screwed Wood down on the contract demanding that work must be completed by 10 June 1862 or pay a penalty of £10 per station per day on any overrun. Our picture was taken on 14 November 1968, 18 months after the station had closed to passengers and about four months after its closure to goods traffic.

This picture at Rowsley was taken on the same day as the previous one. If you look carefully at the station canopy you will see that one of the supporting columns is missing. It had been missing for years; deliberately removed before the Great War so that when Royal visitors alighted here they would be able to walk in a straight line to the station exit.

In 2008 Rowsley South remains the northern terminus of Peak Rail, a society formed in 1975 to reopen the Matlock–Buxton line closed by BR in 1968. The Darley Dale–Rowsley section opened to passengers during 1997 and in the not-too-distant future it is hoped that work on the extension into Bakewell can begin.

It is Monday 25 September 2006, the weekend diesel gala at Peak Rail is over, the visitors have left and the only action involves this diesel-hydraulic shunter, built in 1976 by Thomas Hill of Rotherham and owned by Andrew Briddon, which was pressed into service to move Class 50 Co-Co No.50029 *Renown* at Rowsley South.

Peak Rail's WD150 leaves a trail of smoke and steam in its wake as it runs round its train at Rowsley South. One of nearly 400 similar locomotives ordered by the Ministry of Supply during the Second World War, this particular engine was built by the Tyneside firm of Robert Stephenson & Hawthorn in 1944. During its government career WD150 had a number of postings, the last being at the Central Ammunition Depot, Kineton. Declared surplus to requirement on the arrival of diesel shunter at Kineton, WD150 was placed into store, remaining there until September 1963 when it was purchased along with 13 classmates by the Hunslet Engine Co. of Leeds. Hunslet had been carrying out experiments to enhance steam locomotive performance and the outcome was the plan to rebuild these engines and offer them for resale. Unfortunately these rebuildings coincided with a glut of fairly new diesel shunters being declared surplus by BR, and WD150 was left on Hunslet's hands. Eventually it was bought by a private buyer, J.D.Warrington, and moved to the Dinting Railway Centre near Glossop and renamed *Warrington*. When Dinting closed in 1990 *Warrington* was purchased by Peak Rail as she was powerful enough to haul five coach passenger trains. In 2003 Peak Rail restored the 0-6-0ST to War Department livery and later renamed it *Royal Pioneer*, a name it had carried when serving at the Royal Engineers depot at Arncott, Bicester. (Clive Hardy)

Diesels No's. 85049 and 85051 were among the smallest owned by BR working on the narrow gauge system at Chesterton Junction Permanent Way Depot. They are pictured here with a locomotive at the other end of the scale; one of BR's famous Deltics *Gordon Highlander* built to haul high speed passenger trains on the East Coast Main Line.

HISTORIC EYAM, SCENE OF THE GREAT 17TH CENTURY PLAGUE.
MIDLAND ROUTE, LIVERPOOL - MANCHESTER & LONDON.

Keen to promote the tourist potential of their line through the Peak, the advertising department of the Midland Railway regularly sent photographers to the likes of Matlock, Bakewell, Buxton, Haddon Hall, Chatsworth House, Castleton, Eyam and so on. Pictures taken between 1885 and 1896 formed the subject material for the department's poster artwork and a series of postcards. At the time the available printing processes and the absence of colour photography meant that these postcards had to be created from original artwork. Up to the outbreak of the Great War some of the best colour printing was done in Germany and the Monsal Dale Viaduct card was in fact printed in Saxony.

The Midland didn't limit its marketing to the UK. In the wake of the Entente Cordiale of April 1904, the advertising department had posters printed in Paris such as "Midland Railway D'Angletterre" as well as the guide book *Chemins de Fer Midland Gare St Pancras Londres*.

CHATSWORTH HOUSE.
FRENCH GARDENS.
MIDLAND ROUTE
LIVERPOOL-MANCHESTER & LONDON.

THE VIADUCT, MONSAL DALE.

HADDON HALL.
THE TERRACE.
MIDLAND ROUTE
LIVERPOOL, MANCHESTER & LONDON

Ordered by the LNER in 1936 from Cowans Sheldon Ltd of Carlisle, this 96-ton steam crane with a 36-ton lift capability spent the last 18 years of its main line career based at Toton until withdrawn from service by BR in March 1988. Throughout much of the 1980s it had acted as spare to Toton's much larger and more powerful diesel breakdown crane, though in May 1984 the old steamer was fired up and used to re-rail a derailed HST train that had come to grief at Clay Cross Junction. The crane arrived at Peak Rail in August 1989,

though it wasn't until 1999 that repairs to bring it up to operational condition commenced. It was steamed for the first time in preservation in February 2000.

Buxton-based Stanier 8F 2-8-0 No.48369 heads a Chaddesden Sidings-bound freight through Bakewell on 18 May 1966. (C.M. & J.M.Bentley)

The main building at Bakewell Station paid host to royalty on many occasions, but by the late 1970s it had been reduced to a coal merchant's yard.

This picture of Hassop station is dated 14 December 1942 and with passenger services having been withdrawn the previous August the station buildings were up for letting. Goods traffic continued and was the usual mixture of coal for domestic use and for Baslow gas works, grain, livestock and animal feed.

Hassop Station was just over a mile north of Bakewell, but until the opening of the Hope Valley line in 1894 it attracted passengers and freight from a wide area including; Great and Little Longstone, Ashford, Pilsley, Calver and Baslow. One of the more unusual aspects of its history concerns the local track gang that worked between Hassop and Bakewell. In 1880 ganger Isaiah Gilbert began trimming a number of hawthorn bushes into animal and bird shapes and though topiary was a relatively common signature among Scottish track gangs, it was unusual in England. At its height the Hassop–Bakewell gang kept 15 bushes trimmed.

Having just come through the 533-yard-long Headstone Tunnel, a north bound goods train rattles over the elegant curved structure that is Monsal Dale Viaduct. The picture taken from Monsal Head is thought to date from a couple of years or so prior to the outbreak of the Great War. (C.M. & J.M.Bentley)

Monsal Dale Viaduct on 15 February 2008.

The Midland never intended having a station at Monsal Dale and its eventual construction may well have been due to pressure from the owners of nearby Cressbrook Mill. The station opened on 1 September 1866 with its construction costs kept to a minimum: the wooden station building which was second hand from Evesham, the provision of only one station nameboard, and there were no toilets (facilities were later added in 1875). A single goods siding was provided mainly for coal traffic. With the opening of the Monsal Dale spar mine (which can be seen in the top right hand corner of our image) and the installation of a steam engine at Cressbrook Mill, coal traffic increased from four to five wagons a week in 1900 to between 25 and 30 by 1922. The station closed to regular traffic on 10 August 1975, though occasional summer excursion trains continued to call.. This picture is looking in the Bakewell direction.

Possibly designed by architect William Barlow and built by Charles Humphreys as part of a three-station deal including Millers Dale and Buxton, Great Longstone was originally going to be named Thornbridge. With goods traffic being handled at Hassop, receipts were always going to be light and it is quite surprising that the place remained open for as long as it did. Here a handful of happy snappers turn out on 10 September 1962 to capture on film the last scheduled trains to stop there before the station closed.

Originally the Midland Railway had intended to route their London–Manchester main line by way of Buxton, in order to capitalise on the town's increasing popularity among the well-heeled as a watering hole and a place to take the cure. However arch rivals London & North Western succeeded in maintaining its hold on Buxton, forcing the Midland to think again. The outcome was the building of a branch from Millers Dale, raising its status from nothing more than country station serving the local hamlet and Tideswell, to an important junction. Before the Edwardian era was over, Millers Dale's importance had grown to such an extent that it had no less than five platforms.

Stanier Jubilee Class 4-6-0 No.5570 waits the road from Millers Dale. The LMS made a number of changes to the former Midland timetable, including increasing the number of St Pancras–Manchester Central expresses calling here from three to five. However at the same time the East Lancashire Express, the 13.25hrs St Pancras–Manchester Victoria, was axed, as was one Manchester Central–Derby service and the Liverpool–Derby express. The LMS also tinkered with the Buxton trains, increasing the service to 16 'Down' and 15 'Up' trains on weekdays. (C.M. & J.M.Bentley)

BR Britannia Class 7 4-6-2 No.70042 *Lord Roberts* pauses at Millers Dale with a Down express. The BR Standard classes, starting with No.70000 *Britannia* and finishing with No.92220 *Evening Star*, would eventually total 999 locomotives split between 12 classes. These ranged in numerical strength from the solitary Class 8 4-6-2 No.71000 *Duke of Gloucester* to the 251 members of the Class 9 2-10-0. The 55 Britannia Class engines (No's.70000–70054) were built between January 1951 and September 1954 and differed from earlier Pacifics in that they had only two cylinders instead

of three or four. But they were designed when Britain was still in the grip of post-war austerity measures and this factor undoubtedly influenced things. Though designed as mixed traffic engines they spent much of their careers working express passenger trains. Withdrawals began in June 1965 with No.70007 *Coeur-de-Lion* and ended with No.70013 *Oliver Cromwell* in August 1968. *Duke of Gloucester* was unique among BR standards in that it was the only one built with three cylinders. (C.M. & J.M.Bentley)

Stanier 8F 2-8-0 No.48451 and a Hughes 'Crab' 2-6-0 rattle through Millers Dale with a mineral train. (C.M. & J.M.Bentley)

On a bleak-looking 23 January 1965, the 10.25hrs Manchester Central–London pulls into Millers Dale Station. (Baz Blood)

A slight detour here to Topley Pike on the old line between Millers Dale and Buxton.

For a number of years Tarmac and Peakstone operated a joint 1,400-ton limestone supertrain usually consisting of 38-four-wheel wagons. The train was scheduled to depart Topley Pike at 14.15hrs for Peak Forest where it was stabled until around 05.00hrs the following morning when it departed for either Widnes or Pendleton. (Baz Blood)

Back to the main line again. North-bound trains on the Derby–Manchester main line faced an almost continuous uphill climb from Rowsley to Peak Forest, some of it at 1 in 90. This meant that heavy freights were often banked for most of the way as shown here as an unidentified 8F 2-8-0 does the honours at the rear of a stone train. Even in the early 1990s when the main line had long since faded into memory, Class 37 diesel-electric locomotives were still performing banking duties for stone trains out of Tunstead and Peak Forest. By about 1993, rationalisation had reduced the number of bankers to one, which spent much of the day up at Peak Forest, dropping into Tunstead as and when required to bank the Northwich hopper services. Having only one banker to play with could cause a few hiccups with the service especially at Tunstead. Most mornings would find one, two, or sometimes three sets of empty Northwich hoppers sitting on the Through Goods Road which lies between Great Rocks Junction and Peak Forest signal boxes and usually at least one of these sets would be needed urgently in Tunstead for loading. Normally the banker went straight to Peak Forest but if he got the chance the signaller at Great Rocks would hijack it to clear the Goods Road. The signaller at Great Rocks Junction controls trains going on to the Through Goods Road. In busier times the Hindlows were recessed here for running round. This move kept the 'Up' main free, allowing other traffic to pass while the run-round was taking place. If the signaller at Peak Forest wants to put a train or loco on the Through Goods Road from his end, he has to check with Great Rocks beforehand. (Baz Blood)

One of Buxton's Class 47 diesel-electrics stands in Tunstead at the head of a rake of ICI hoppers. Introduced from 1936 onwards, the 43.5-ton ICI bogie hopper proved an outstanding success and their eventual withdrawal from service was more to do with the fact that they were equipped with vacuum rather than modern air-brakes. Delivery of the first 85 hoppers was spread over three years for evaluation purposes, the last 11 of these becoming operational during 1939. A second batch of 35 hoppers was ordered in August 1945. They differed from the original ones in that they had plate frame bogies allowing the carrying capacity to be increased by one ton. A third and final batch of 32 hoppers was ordered in June 1951 for delivery during 1952–53.

Accidents at New Mills and Hartford resulted in a number being cut up but the fleet was brought back up to strength during 1983 when 13 similar vehicles were bought from John Summers Steelworks. Aside from the accidents, they proved pretty well indestructible, but with BR keen to do away with vacuum-braked rolling stock, the original prototype hopper was experimentally fitted with air brakes in 1986. Proposals were made to refit the fleet with new air-braked bogies, but it never went ahead and the hoppers continued in service.

During the early 1990s, trials were also carried out with air-braked vehicles supplied by Tiphook Rail.

The Tiphooks were put through their paces on a series of trains to Hindlow and back, but it soon became apparent that these modern vehicles lacked the armoured resilience of the old hoppers, especially when tons of three inch stone was dropped in them from a great height in Tunstead. The old hoppers had simply bounced around a bit on their well-sprung bogies. The Tiphooks, on the other hand, began to part company with their frames which had to be welded back in place. The old ICI hoppers remained in service until replaced by new 102-ton vehicles ordered by Buxton Lime Industries. (Baz Blood)

The first ever 6E56 Tunstead–Drax working to be hauled by a National Power-owned locomotive stands ready on 26 April 1994. Though before it can roll, Driver Baz Blood (seen here happily posing for posterity) will have to scamper across the other side of his cab as that is where the controls are. At the time No.59201 *Vale of York* was the only main line engine National Power possessed, though others were on order and the company had invested heavily in a traction maintenance depot at Ferry Bridge. Arriving at Tunstead

early on Monday morning No.59201 was then effectively out-based at the quarry until the following Friday, when after working that day's train to Drax, it would proceed to Ferry Bridge for weekend maintenance, with the cycle starting again the following Monday. National Power eventually sold its railway operating interests to EWS. (Baz Blood)

Preserved 8F 2-8-0 No.48151 eases towards Causeway Tunnel in Buxton Lime Industries' Tunstead Quarry complex during celebrations marking the 60th anniversary of the introduction of the Northwich hopper fleet. (Baz Blood)

The crew of Stanier 8F 2-8-0 No.48605 work up a thirst taking their charge for a spin on the turntable at Great Rocks Junction. Note the slats around the turntable to enable them to get a good grip with their boots. (C.M. & J.M.Bentley)

This picture, taken from the road bridge at Great Rocks Junction on Sunday, 24 September 2006, looks up the 1 in 9 incline towards Peak Forest. The locomotives, predominantly Class 60 diesel-electrics built by Brush Traction at Loughborough in the 1990s, are stabled in the engine holding sidings situated behind Peak Forest signal box. In BR days, locomotives were stabled at Buxton, but since privatisation the depot has closed and a fuelling point installed at Peak Forest. The tracks, from left to right, are: the Through Goods Road, 'Up' main and 'Down' main; while the two sidings to the right are used for drawing down or stabling ore trains from the RMC quarry.

Stanier Black 5 No.44890 stands at
Peak Forest station at the head of a
rake of ICI hoppers awaiting a path
into Tunstead. (Baz Blood)

1Co-Co1 Class 40 No.40150 passes the abandoned hulk of the Smalldale crusher plant on 11 August 1983. Dating from 1919, the crusher fell into disuse and its equipment was removed after Tunstead No.2 crusher came on line during 1946, though for a while this vast building housed an experimental kiln.

When first operational, Smalldale's two crushers turned out stone to a maximum diameter of 8inches with stone up to 2.5inches being sold as gravel. In 1921 a drying and grinding plant was opened nearby enabling the gravel to be reduced down to dust. (Baz Blood)

EWS Class 60 No.60015 stands at RMC's Peak Forest quarry on Sunday 24 September 2006. Parked up over on the right are 350hp Class 08 0-6-0DE No.08588 and one of RMC's diesel-hydraulics. (Clive Hardy)

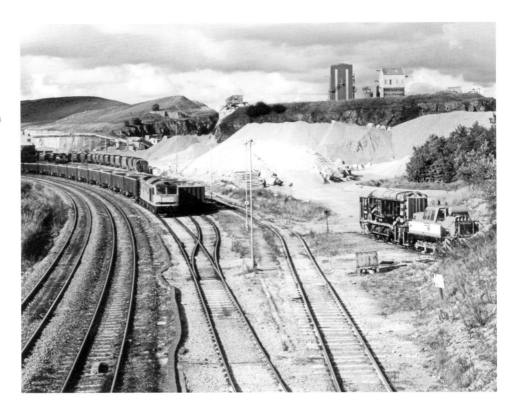

MANCHESTER, CHINLEY, HATHERSAGE and SHEFFIELD

Miles		Week Days am	am	am	am	am	pm S	pm	pm EC	pm P	pm S	pm	pm	pm P	Sundays am	am P	pm	pm	pm	pm
	Manchester (Cen.) .... dep	..	6 5	..	9 0	1125	..	1 55	2 50	4 3	4 32	5 55	7 30	9 30	9 0	1010	2 0	..	6 0	7 30
	Stockport (T.D.) ...... "	..	6 34	..	8 52	11 9	..	1 35	3 42	4 29	4 50	5F37	7T45	9 55	8 52	1035	2 30	..	5 33	..
20	Chinley ...... "	7 5	7 40	..	9 43	1215	..	2C31	4 23	5 11	5 40	6 33	8 30	1046	9 55	1112	3 20	..	6 42	8 15
25¾	Edale	7 18	7 53	..	9 56	1229	..	2C46	4 36	5 24	5 53	6 46	8 43	11 0	10 9	1126	3 34	..	6 56	8 29
30½	Hope A	7 26	8 2	9 0	10 4	1237	1 30	2C54	4 44	5 32	6 1	6 54	8 51	11 8	1017	1134	3 42	6 35	7 4	8 37
32½	Bamford	7 30	8 6	9 3	10 8	1241	1 33	2C58	4 48	5 36	6 5	6 58	8 55	1112	1021	1138	3 46	6 38	7 9	8 41
34¼	Hathersage	7 34	8 10	9 9	1012	1246	1 37	3C 3	4 52	5 40	6 9	7 2	8 59	1117	1026	1143	3 51	6 43	7 15	8 46
36½	Grindleford	7 39	8 15	9 14	1017	1251	1 42	3C 8	4 57	5 45	6 14	7 7	9 4	1122	1031	1148	3 56	6 48	7 20	8 51
41¼	Dore and Totley	7 49	8 24	9 23	1026	1 0	..	3C17	5 6	5 54	6 23	7 16	9 13	1131	1040	..	4 5	6 57	7 29	9 0
49¼	247Chesterfield (Mid.) .. arr	8 10	8 47	..	1258	1S30	..	4 37	6 0	6 22	..	7 49	9 46	..	..	..	4 26	..	..	..
71	234Mansfield (Town) 234a "	..	..	..	..	..	..	..	..	..	..	..	..	..	..	..	..	..	..	..
42	Beauchief	..	..	..	..	..	..	3C20	5 9	5 57	..	7 19	..	..	..	..	..	..	..	..
42¾	Millhouses & Ecclesall	7 53	..	9 27	1030	1 4	..	3C23	5 12	6 0	6 27	7 22	9 17	..	1044	..	4 9	7 1	7 33	9 4
44	Heeley	7 57	8 30	9 31	1034	1 8	1 55	3C27	5 16	6 4	6 31	7 26	9 21	1137	1048	..	4 13	7 5	7 37	9 8
45½	Sheffield (Mid.) ...... arr	8 4	8 35	9 36	1039	1 13	2 0	3C32	5 21	6 9	6 36	7 31	9 26	1142	1053	12 3	4 18	7 10	7 42	9 13
51	247Rotherham (Mas.) .. arr	8‡23	8 53	10C14	11 28	1 54	2 40	4 24	5 41	6 55	6 55	8 47	9 44	1a39	..	1234	6 24	7 39	8 19	9 33

Miles		Week Days am	am	am	am P	am	am S	am	pm S	pm	pm P	pm E	pm	pm	Sundays am	am	am	am P	pm P	pm P	pm
	247Rotherham (Mas.) .. dep	4 39	..	7‡18	..	1018	1111	1111	1 28	3 28	5J10	5 36	6 43	8 40	4 7	..	8 30	8 30	1 20	5 48	6 24
—	Sheffield (Mid.) ...... dep	6 5	7 2	7 42	8 5	1055	1225	1250	2 22	4 30	5 30	6 0	7 7	9 24	8 30	9 0	9 30	10 0	2 0	6 10	7 0
1¼	Heeley	6 9	7 7	7 46	..	1059	1239	1254	2 26	4 34	5 35	6 4	7 11	9 28	8 35	9 5	9 35	10 5	2 6	6 15	..
2¼	Millhouses & Ecclesall	..	7 13	7 51	..	11 4	..	1258	2 31	4 39	5 41	6 9	7 16	..	8 41	9 11	..	1011	2 12	6 21	..
3¼	Beauchief	..	..	7 54	..	11 7	..	1 2	2 34	4 42	..	..	..	..	..	..	..	..	..	..	..
—	234aMansfield (Town) 234 dep	..	..	..	..	..	..	..	..	..	..	..	..	..	..	..	..	..	..	..	..
—	247Chesterfield (Mid.) .. "	..	6 56	7 25	..	..	..	..	1 59	3 57	5 17	5 48	..	8 40	7 57	..	..	..	..	..	..
4¼	Dore and Totley	6 18	7 20	7 58	..	1110	1247	1 5	2 37	4 45	5 47	6 14	7 21	9 36	8 50	9 18	..	1017	2 19	6 27	..
9¼	Grindleford	6 30	7 32	8 9	..	1121	1258	1 16	2 48	4 56	5 59	6 25	7 32	9 47	9 2	9 30	9 54	1029	2 31	6 39	7 21
11¾	Hathersage	6 35	7 37	8 14	..	1126	1 7	1 21	2 50	5 1	6 4	6 30	7 37	9 42	9 8	9 37	9 59	1034	2 36	6 44	7 26
13	Bamford	6 40	7 42	8 18	..	1130	1 11	1 25	2 57	5 5	6 9	6 34	7 41	9 56	9 13	9 42	10 4	1039	2 41	6 49	7 31
14¾	Hope A	6 47	7 48	8 24	8 32	1136	1 17	1 31	3 5	5 11	6 15	6 40	7 47	10 2	9 20	9 48	1010	1045	2 47	6 56	7 37
19¾	Edale	6 59	8 1	..	8 44	1148	..	1 43	3 15	5 23	6 28	6 52	7 59	1014	9 33	10 1	..	1058	3 0	7 9	7 50
25¼	Chinley ...... arr	7 11	8 13	..	8 55	12 0	..	1 55	3 27	5 35	6 40	7 4	8 11	1026	9 45	1013	..	1110	3 12	7 21	8 2
37¼	Stockport (T.D.) ...... "	7H50	8L42	..	9Z39	1Y22	..	3H 1	..	6N41	7 17	..	8 57	1114	..	..	..	1157	3 58	7 53	8 42
45½	Manchester (Cen.) ..... "	8 8	9 0	..	9 23	1 5	..	2 30	..	6 30	7 45	..	8 50	11 8	..	..	..	1222	4 23	8 18	8 45

Y 3 minutes later on Saturdays
Z Passengers can arr **Cheadle Heath** (Stockport) 9 54 am

A For Castleton (2 miles) and Bradwell
a am
C Through Carriages Stockport to Sheffield
Ȼ Arr 9 50 am on Saturdays
E or E Except Saturdays
F Except Saturdays. **Cheadle Heath** (Stockport). Passengers can dep Tiviot Dale 4 50 pm (daily)
H **Cheadle Heath** (Stockport)
J Dep 4 30 pm on Saturdays
K Runs 2 minutes *earlier* on Saturdays
L **Cheadle Heath** (Stockport). Passengers can arr Tiviot Dale 8 51 am
N Passengers can arr **Cheadle Heath** (Stockport) at 6 13 pm
P Through Carriages between Manchester and Sheffield
S or S Saturdays only
T **Cheadle Heath** (Stockport). Passengers can dep Tiviot Dale 7 16 pm
‡ Arr 3 39 pm on Saturdays

BUXTON and MILLER'S DALE

Miles		Week Days am	am	am	am T	am	am	pm	pm	pm	pm	pm	pm	pm E	pm	pm	pm	pm	pm S	Sundays am	am	am	pm	pm	pm	pm	pm	pm	pm	pm	pm
	Buxton ...... dep	7 55	8 16	8 46	9 42	1025	1130	12 2	1 30	2 25	4 3	4 36	5 15	5 50	6 35	7 40	8 24	10 0	1045	8 30	9 45	1020	1250	2 45	3 25	6 30	6 40	7 15	7 30	8 20	9 50
5¼	Miller's Dale ...... arr	8 4	8 25	8 55	9 51	1034	1139	1211	1 39	2 34	4 12	4 45	5 24	5 59	6 44	7 49	8 33	10 9	1054	8 39	9 54	1029	1259	2 54	3 34	6 39	6 49	7 24	7 39	8 29	9 59

Miles		Week Days am	am	am	am	am	am	pm	pm	pm	pm E	pm	pm	pm	pm T	pm	pm	pm	pm	ngt S	Sundays am	am	am	am	pm	pm	pm	pm	pm	pm	pm	pm
	Miller's Dale ...... dep	8 0	8 18	8 38	9 10	1010	1048	1225	1240	1 55	2 27	2 54	4 18	5 0	5 58	7 0	8 7	8 55	1025	1212	8 55	10 7	1045	1154	1 16	3 7	3 50	5 55	7 8	7 54	8 45	1020
5¼	Buxton ...... arr	8 10	8 28	8 48	9 20	1020	1058	1235	1253	2 5	2 37	3 4	4 28	5 10	6 8	7 10	8 17	9 5	1035	1222	9 5	1017	1055	12 4	1 26	3 17	4 0	6 5	7 18	8 4	8 55	1030

E Except Saturdays. **S** Saturdays only. **T** Through Carriages to and from London (Table 211)

DERBY, MATLOCK, BUXTON, CHINLEY, STOCKPORT and MANCHESTER

Week Days

Miles from Derby	Station	am		am	am		am	am	am		am	am	am		am	am	am	am		am	am		am		am		pm	pm
							Except Saturdays						Forms 9 5 am Chinley to Manchester (Cen.)				TC London to Manchester	Continuation of 7 10 am from Derby (Midland)			TC Nottingham to Liverpool (Cen.)		Forms 12 50 pm Chinley to Manchester (Cen.)		RC London to Derby (Midland) except Saturdays; TC London to Manchester			Continuation of 10 20 am from Derby (Midland)
	208 London (St. Pancras) dep	..	..	..	..	..	..	..	..	..	..	..	..	..	..	..	4 15	..	..	..	..	..	..	..	8 15	..	..	..
	208 Kettering "	..	..	..	..	..	..	..	..	..	..	..	..	..	..	..	6T24	..	..	..	7 15	..	7 15	..	9T53	..	..	..
	208 Leicester (Lon. Rd.) "	..	..	..	..	..	..	..	..	..	..	..	..	..	..	..	7T13	..	..	..	8 37	..	8 37	..	10T39	..	..	..
	208 Loughborough (M.) "	..	..	..	..	..	..	..	..	..	..	..	..	..	..	..	7T30	..	..	..	9 1	..	9 1	..	10T57	..	..	..
	236 Mansfield (Town) "	..	..	..	..	..	..	..	..	..	..	..	..	..	..	..	5 40	..	..	..	7 53	..	7 53	..	9N 3	..	..	..
	233 Nottingham (Mid.) "	..	..	..	..	..	..	..	..	..	..	..	..	..	..	..	7 0	..	..	..	9 6	..	9 6	..	10 30	..	..	..
	210 Bristol (T.M.) "	..	..	..	..	..	..	..	..	..	..	..	1 10	..	..	..	..	..	..	..	..	..	..	..	7 35	..	..	..
	210 Birmingham (N.St.) "	..	..	..	..	..	..	..	..	..	..	..	4 28	..	..	6 40	6 40	..	..	..	8 5	..	9 0	..	10 11	..	..	..
	210 Tamworth (H.L.) "	..	..	..	..	..	..	..	..	..	..	..	4 55	..	..	7 11	7 11	..	..	..	8 38	..	9 31	..	..	..	..	..
—	Derby (Midland) dep	..	..	..	..	..	..	..	..	..	..	..	7 10	..	..	7 58	8 10	..	..	..	9 44	..	10 20	..	11 25	..	..	..
¾	Derby (Nottingham Road)	..	..	..	..	..	..	..	..	..	..	..	..	..	..	..	..	..	..	..	..	..	..	..	..	..	..	..
5½	Duffield	..	..	..	..	..	..	..	..	..	..	..	7 19	..	..	8 8	..	..	..	..	..	..	10 29	..	..	..	..	..
7¾	Belper	..	..	..	..	..	..	..	..	..	..	..	7 25	..	..	8 14	..	..	..	..	9 56	..	10 36	..	..	..	..	..
—	247 Chesterfield (Mid.) dep	..	..	..	..	..	..	..	..	..	..	..	6 38	..	..	..	..	..	..	..	..	..	8 50	..	..	..	..	..
10½	Ambergate	..	..	..	..	..	..	..	..	..	..	..	7 31	..	..	8 20	8 25	..	..	..	..	..	10 43	..	..	..	..	..
12½	Whatstandwell	..	..	..	..	..	..	..	..	..	..	..	7 36	..	..	..	..	..	..	..	..	..	10 48	..	..	..	..	..
15½	Cromford	..	..	..	..	..	..	..	..	..	..	..	7 43	..	..	..	..	..	..	..	..	..	10 55	..	..	..	..	..
16	Matlock Bath	..	..	..	..	..	..	..	..	..	..	..	7 47	..	..	..	..	..	..	..	..	..	10 59	..	..	..	..	..
17	Matlock	..	..	..	..	..	..	..	..	..	..	..	7 52	..	..	..	8 36	..	..	..	10 12	..	11 4	..	11 49	..	..	..
19½	Darley Dale	..	..	..	..	..	..	..	..	..	..	..	7 58	..	..	..	..	..	..	..	..	..	11 10	..	..	..	..	..
21½	Rowsley B	..	..	..	..	..	..	..	..	..	..	..	8 4	..	..	..	..	..	..	..	10 26	..	11 16	..	..	..	..	..
24½	Bakewell D	..	..	..	..	..	..	..	..	..	..	..	8 12	..	..	..	..	..	..	..	..	..	11 24	..	..	..	..	..
27½	Great Longstone F	..	..	..	..	..	..	..	..	..	..	..	8 18	..	..	..	..	..	..	..	..	..	11 30	..	..	..	..	..
28½	Monsal Dale	..	..	..	..	..	..	..	..	..	..	..	8 23	..	..	..	..	..	..	..	..	..	11 35	..	..	..	..	..
31½	Miller's Dale G arr	..	..	..	..	..	..	..	..	..	..	..	8 30	..	..	..	9 2	..	..	..	10 39	..	11 42	..	12 15	..	..	..
36¾	Buxton arr	..	..	..	..	..	..	..	..	..	..	..	8 48	..	..	..	9 20	..	..	..	10 58	..	12 35	..	12 35	..	..	..
	Buxton dep	..	..	7 5	..	..	..	..	..	..	..	8 0	8 16	..	..	..	8 46	..	..	9 15	10 25	..	11 30	..	12 2	..	..	..
—	Miller's Dale dep	..	..	..	..	..	..	..	..	..	..	..	8 32	..	..	..	9 5	..	..	..	10 41	..	11 44	..	12 17	..	..	..
35¾	Peak Forest, for Peak Dale	..	..	7 18	..	..	..	..	..	..	..	8 13	8 43	..	..	..	..	..	..	..	..	..	11 56	..	..	..	..	..
39¼	Chapel-en-le-Frith (Central)	..	..	7 27	..	..	..	..	..	..	..	8 21	8 50	..	..	..	..	..	..	9 34	..	..	12 4	..	..	..	..	..
41½	Chinley arr	..	..	7 32	..	..	..	..	..	..	..	8 26	8 55	..	..	..	..	..	..	9 38	11 1	..	12 9	..	12 37	..	..	..
	Chinley dep	..	..	7 34	..	..	..	..	..	..	8 18	8 29	..	..	8 58	..	..	9 5	..	9 40	11 3	..	..	..	12 39	..	..	12J50
42½	Buxworth	..	..	7 36	..	..	..	..	..	..	8 20	..	..	..	..	..	..	9 7	..	..	..	..	..	..	..	..	..	12J52
45¼	New Mills (Central)	..	..	..	..	..	..	..	..	..	8 28	..	..	..	..	..	..	9 15	..	..	..	..	..	..	..	..	..	1J 0
46¾	Strines	..	..	..	..	..	..	..	..	..	8 34	..	..	..	..	..	..	9 21	..	..	..	..	..	..	..	..	..	1J 6
48¾	Marple	..	..	..	..	..	..	..	..	..	8 40	..	..	..	..	..	..	9 27	..	..	..	..	..	..	..	..	..	1J11
50½	Romiley	..	..	..	..	..	..	..	..	..	8 44	..	..	..	..	..	..	9 32	..	..	..	..	..	..	..	..	..	1J15
53¾	Stockport (T. Dale) arr	..	..	..	..	..	..	..	..	..	8 51	..	..	..	..	..	..	9 39	..	..	..	..	..	..	..	..	..	1J22
	Stockport (T. Dale) dep	..	..	..	..	..	..	8 21	..	..	8 52	..	..	..	..	..	..	9 40	..	..	..	..	..	..	..	..	..	1J24
53½	Cheadle Heath, Stockport	7 0	..	7 51	7 58	..	8 14	..	8 31	..	..	8 43	..	..	..	..	..	..	..	9 55	..	..	..	..	..	..	1 2	..
54½	Heaton Mersey	7 3	..	..	8 1	..	8 17	8 26	8 34	..	8 58	..	..	..	..	..	..	9 46	..	..	..	..	..	..	..	..	1 5	1J30
55¾	Didsbury	7 6	..	..	8 4	..	8 20	8 29	8 37	..	9 2	..	..	..	..	..	..	9 49	..	..	..	..	..	..	..	..	1 8	1J34
56½	Withington & W. Didsbury	7 9	..	..	8 7	..	8 23	8 33	8 40	..	9 5	..	..	..	..	..	..	9 52	..	..	..	..	..	..	..	..	1 11	1J37
58¼	Chorlton-cum-Hardy	7 14	..	..	8 12	..	8 28	8 38	8 45	..	9 10	..	..	..	..	..	..	9 57	..	..	..	..	..	..	..	..	1 16	1J42
61½	Manchester (Central) arr	7 23	..	8 8	8 22	..	8 37	8 47	8 54	..	9 19	9 0	..	..	9 23	..	9 49	10 6	..	10 9	11 29	..	..	..	1 5	..	1 25	1J51
95½	150 Liverpool (Central) arr	8 44	..	9 15	9 15	..	..	..	..	..	..	..	..	..	1015	..	1046	1115	..	1115	1220	..	..	..	2 15	..	3 15	3 15

Week Days—continued

Station	am	pm		am	am		pm	am	pm	pm	pm	pm	pm	pm	pm	pm		pm	pm	pm		pm	pm	pm	
	Saturdays only	Saturdays only		RC and TC London to Manchester	Except Saturdays		Except Saturdays	Saturdays only	Except Saturdays	Forms 6 9 pm Chinley to Manchester (Cen.)	TC London to Buxton and Manchester (Cen.)	RC London to Derby		Continuation of 4 10 pm from Derby (Midland)				RC and TC London to Manchester				RC London to Derby (Midland); TC to London Manchester		Saturdays only	
208 London (St. Pancras) dep	8 15	..	..	10 15	10 15	..	..	1015	..	12N25	2 25	2 25	..	..	..	..	..	4 15	..	4 15	..	6 40	..	7 10	..
208 Kettering "	9 53	..	..	11R36	11 36	..	..	1136	..	1N30	2d43	2d43	..	..	..	..	..	5R44	..	5 44	..	8T 0	..	8 38	..
208 Leicester (Lon. Rd.) "	1039	..	..	12R13	12p13	..	..	1213	..	2N 4	4T15	4 15	..	..	..	..	..	6R23	..	6 23	..	8T38	..	8 38	..
208 Loughborough (M.) "	1057	..	..	12R28	12 28	..	..	1228	..	12 57	3 53	3 53	..	..	..	..	..	6U 1	..	6U 1	..	8T55	..	8 55	..
236 Mansfield (Town) "	9 30	..	..	..	..	..	..	..	..	1 2	1E14	1E14	..	..	..	..	..	4 55	..	4 55	..	6 20	..	8 53	..
233 Nottingham (Mid.) "	11 5	..	..	11a49	11a49	..	..	1149	..	2K 0	4 10	4 10	..	..	..	..	..	6 9	..	6 [illegible]	..	8 30	..	9 55	..
210 Bristol (T.M.) "	7 35	..	..	8 45	8 45	..	..	8 45	..	12 30	1230	1230	..	..	2 15	..	..	2 15	..	2 15	..	4 45	..	4 45	..
210 Birmingham (N.St.) "	1011	..	..	11 39	11 39	..	..	1139	..	3 5	3 5	3 5	..	..	4 42	..	..	5 15	..	5 15	..	7 18	..	9 0	..
210 Tamworth (H.L.) "	..	..	..	12 3	12 3	..	..	12 3	..	2 9	2 9	2 9	..	..	5 5	..	..	5 59	..	5 59	..	7 42	..	9 52	..
Derby (Midland) dep	1220	..	..	12p55	1p 5	..	..	1p 5	..	4 10	4 53	5 5	..	..	5 50	..	..	7 6	..	7 16	..	9 27	..	1057	..
Derby (Nottingham Road)	1222	..	..	..	..	..	..	..	..	..	..	..	..	..	5E52	..	..	..	..	..	..	..	..	..	..
Duffield	1231	..	..	..	1 14	..	..	1 14	..	4 19	..	..	..	..	6 3	..	..	..	..	7 25	..	..	..	11 6	..
Belper	1237	..	..	..	1 20	..	..	1 20	..	4 25	..	5 17	..	..	6 10	..	..	..	..	7 33	..	..	..	1112	..
247 Chesterfield (Mid.) dep	..	..	..	..	..	..	..	..	..	..	..	..	..	..	4 39	..	..	..	..	6 2	..	..	..	9 51	..
Ambergate	1243	..	..	..	1 27	..	..	1 27	..	4 31	..	..	..	..	6 16	..	..	..	..	7 39	..	..	..	1118	..
Whatstandwell	1248	..	..	..	1 32	..	..	1 32	..	4 36	..	5 26	..	..	6 21	..	..	..	..	7 44	..	..	..	1123	..
Cromford	1255	..	..	..	1 39	..	..	1 39	..	4 43	..	5 33	..	..	6 28	..	..	..	..	7 51	..	..	..	1130	..
Matlock Bath	1259	..	..	..	1 43	..	..	1 43	..	4 47	..	5 37	..	..	6 32	..	..	..	..	7 55	..	..	..	1134	..
Matlock	1 3	..	..	1 18	1 47	..	..	1 47	..	4 51	..	5 41	..	..	6 36	..	..	7 30	..	8 0	..	9 51	..	1138	..
Darley Dale	1 9	..	..	..	1 53	..	..	1 53	..	4 56	..	5 47	..	..	6 42	..	..	..	..	8 5	..	..	..	1143	..
Rowsley B	..	..	..	..	2 0	..	..	2 0	..	5 1	..	5 53	..	..	..	..	..	..	..	8 10	..	..	..	1148	..
Bakewell D	..	..	..	..	2 8	..	..	2 8	..	5 9	..	6 1	..	..	..	..	..	..	..	8 18	..	..	..	1156	..
Great Longstone F	..	..	..	..	2 14	..	..	2 14	..	5 15	..	..	..	..	..	..	..	..	..	8 24	..	..	..	12 2	..
Monsal Dale	..	..	..	..	2 18	..	..	2 18	..	5 19	..	..	..	..	..	..	..	..	..	8S28	..	..	..	..	..
Miller's Dale G arr	..	..	..	1 42	2 25	..	..	2 25	..	5 26	5 35	..	..	..	..	..	..	7 56	..	8 35	..	1016	..	1210	..
Buxton arr	..	..	..	2 5	2 37	..	..	3 4	..	6 8	6 8	..	..	..	..	..	..	8 17	..	9 5	..	1035	..	1222	..
Buxton dep	..	1 25	..	1 30	..	..	..	2 25	..	5 15	5 15	..	..	..	..	..	..	7 40	..	8 24	..	10 0	..	..	..
Miller's Dale dep	..	..	..	1 44	..	..	..	2 37	..	5 28	5 39	..	..	..	..	..	..	7 59	..	8 39	..	1017	..	..	..
Peak Forest, for Peak Dale	..	1 38	..	..	..	..	..	2 49	..	5 39	..	..	..	..	..	..	..	..	..	8 51	..	..	..	..	..
Chapel-en-le-Frith (Central)	..	1 46	..	..	..	..	..	2 57	..	5 46	..	..	..	..	..	..	..	..	..	9 0	..	..	..	..	..
Chinley arr	..	1 51	..	2 3	..	..	..	3 2	..	5 51	5 58	..	..	..	..	..	..	8 19	..	9 5	..	1037	..	..	..
Chinley dep	..	..	..	2 5	..	..	2 28	3 6	..	..	6 0	..	..	6 9	..	6 47	..	8 21	8 30	9 8	..	1039	1046	..	..
Buxworth	..	..	..	..	..	..	2 30	3 8	..	..	..	..	..	6 11	..	6 49	..	..	..	9 10	..	..	..	..	..
New Mills (Central)	..	..	..	..	..	..	2 38	3 16	..	..	..	..	..	6 21	..	6 57	..	..	8 38	9 18	..	..	1054	..	..
Strines	..	..	..	..	..	..	2 44	3 22	..	..	..	..	..	..	..	..	..	..	..	..	..	..	..	..	..
Marple	..	..	..	..	..	..	2 49	3 27	..	..	..	..	..	6 29	..	7 5	..	..	8 46	9 26	..	..	11 3	..	..
Romiley	..	..	..	..	..	..	2 54	3 32	..	..	..	..	..	6 34	..	7 10	..	..	8 50	9 30	..	..	11 7	..	..
Stockport (T. Dale) arr	..	..	..	..	..	..	3 1	3 39	..	..	..	..	..	6 41	..	7 17	..	..	8 57	9 37	..	..	1114	..	..
Stockport (T. Dale) dep	..	..	..	..	..	..	..	3 40	..	..	..	..	..	6 42	..	7 18	..	..	8 58	9 38	..	..	1115	..	..
Cheadle Heath, Stockport	..	..	..	..	..	..	..	..	5 31	..	6 14	..	6 35	..	..	..	..	..	..	..	..	..	..	..	..
Heaton Mersey	..	..	..	..	..	..	..	3 46	5 34	..	..	..	6 38	6 48	..	7 24	..	..	9 4	9 44	..	..	..	..	..
Didsbury	..	..	..	..	..	..	..	3 50	5 37	..	..	..	6 42	6 52	..	7 28	..	Vv	9 8	9 48	..	Zz	1122	..	..
Withington & W. Didsbury	..	..	..	..	..	..	..	3 53	5 40	..	..	..	6 45	6 55	..	7 31	..	..	9 11	9 51	..	..	..	..	..
Chorlton-cum-Hardy	..	..	..	..	..	..	..	3 58	5 45	..	..	..	6 50	7 0	..	7 36	..	..	9 16	9 56	..	..	..	..	..
Manchester (Central) arr	..	..	..	2 30	..	..	..	4 7	5 54	..	6 30	..	6 59	7 9	..	7 45	..	8 50	9 25	10 5	..	11 8	1136	..	..
150 Liverpool (Central) arr	..	..	..	3 26	..	..	..	5 15	7 27	..	8 24	..	8 24	8 24	..	8 52	..	1015	1115	1115	..	..	..	..	..

a am
B Station for Chatsworth (2¾ miles) and Haddon Hall (1¾ miles)
C Arr 12 30 pm on Saturdays
D Station for Haddon Hall (2¼ miles) and Chatsworth (3½ miles)
d 3 minutes later on Saturdays

E Except Saturdays
F Great Longstone for Ashford
G Station for Tideswell (1¾ miles)
E Dep 9 30 am on Saturdays
J 3 minutes later on Saturdays
K Dep 2 5 pm on Saturdays
N Dep St. Pancras 12 18, Kettering 1 20, and Leicester 2 25 pm on Saturdays
p pm

R Refreshment Car and Through Carriages to Manchester
RC Refreshment Car
S or $ Saturdays only
T Through Carriages to Manchester
TC Through Carriages
U Dep 5 34 pm on Saturdays
Vv Stops at 8 37 pm to set down
Zz Stops at 10 55 pm to set down

Harry Townley captured this quiet moment at Chinley on 23 September 1950. As with Millers Dale, this was a large station in the middle of nowhere, but when first opened in the 1860s Chinley was a typical country station with a couple of platforms, a goods shed and a cattle dock. In those days the Midland main line from Derby extended only as far as New Mills from where trains to and from Manchester had to run via the Manchester, Sheffield & Lincolnshire Railway. When the Midland opened its line between New Mills South Junction and Manchester Central, Chinley's fortunes began to look up, especially when it came to goods traffic. The quantum leap however came in 1894 with the opening of the line between Sheffield Midland, the Hope Valley and Vale of Edale to a new junction about a mile to the east of Chinley station. This new line enabled the Midland to compete for traffic against the MS&LR's lucrative Woodhead route but it soon became apparent that Chinley was now an operational bottleneck.

Between 1902 and 1903 the track between Chinley North and New Mills South signal boxes was quadrupled and a new enlarged Chinley Station built just to the west of the original one. The new station had five through platforms, goods sheds and a turntable. Harry's picture is looking towards Sheffield with the station's distinctive footbridge which spanned all six platforms clearly be shown. (C.M. & J.M.Bentley)

2P 4-4-0 No.40486 pauses at Chinley with a 'Down' slow on 4 August 1957. At this period the timetable was pretty much the same as that imposed during the Second World War. Ironically when the axe fell on the Derby–Manchester route its weekday services had been increased to 26 'Down' and 25 'Up' trains. (C.M. & J.M.Bentley)

Chinley signal box was commissioned on 6 December 1982 to replace the old Midland Railway cabin which was demolished soon after.

Engineers begin the task of clearing the wreckage following a collision due to signalling errors between a passenger train and two stationary coupled locomotives at Chinley on the evening of 9 March 1986. The locomotives were standing at a signal on the 'Up' line awaiting the route to be set that would take them across the passenger lines and on to the goods line to Peak Forest and Buxton. Meanwhile, on the 'Down', a locomotive-hauled passenger train had come to a standstill at a signal which the signalman could not clear because a track-circuit had failed, locking the points to the loop line to Buxton.

The signalman got in his car and drove to the points and pumped them over but unfortunately did not secure them in any way. Adding to this error was the fact that ahead of this problem were two other sets of points that were incorrectly set and not locked. The signalman then authorised the driver of the passenger train to proceed but the route now set put him on a collision course with the two locomotives.

On seeing the passenger train approaching at about 30mph the driver of the two locomotives quickly released the brakes and put his engines into reverse; an action that almost certainly reduced the severity of the impact and number of casualties, though alas one passenger was killed. The locomotive No.31436 was found to be so badly damaged that it was withdrawn from service, taken to the British Rail Engineering in Doncaster and cut up for scrap the following December.

The damaged locomotive and coach are being assessed as to whether or not they can be moved by rail. In the background is an engineers train with locomotives at both ends so as to avoid the hassle of running round.

Almost 12 months on and Chinley is the scene of another smash. On a dry, fine afternoon on 20 February 1987 at approximately 16.53hrs, the 14.32hrs Peak Forest–Bletchley freight passed a signal at danger at Chinley North Junction and became derailed. Unfortunately the 16.22 Sheffield to Liverpool passenger train was heading through Chinley under clear signals at about 50mph and crashed into the derailed wagons. Of the 113 passengers on the train, seven were slightly injured as were the driver and guard. Engineers managed to clear away sufficient wreckage to allow one line to be reopened at 08.55hrs on Sunday 22 February.

DINTING

In 1968 the *Bahamas* Locomotive Society were looking around for somewhere to house their newly restored Jubilee Class 4-6-0 express passenger engine when the opportunity arose to acquire a site at Dinting from British Rail. When this picture was taken on 30 October 1975 the society had put in a considerable amount of effort, time and money developing the Dinting Railway Centre so that it could be a base of operations for locomotives cleared for working on BR. The development included building this exhibition hall capable of holding up to nine main line locomotives, of which No.5596 *Bahamas* and former Southern Railway V Class 4-4-0 *Repton* are pictured here.

A close-up of LMS Jubilee Class 4-6-0 No.5690 *Leander* at Dinting on 23 October 1973. Designed by William Stanier, 191 Jubilees were built between 1934 and 1936, of which four were preserved: the North British Locomotive Company's No.5593 *Kolhapur* and No.5596 *Bahamas,* and the Crewe-built No.5690 *Leander* and No.5699 *Galatea.* Of the four, *Bahamas* is most easily recognised as she is fitted with a double chimney.

Leander receives
a spot of TLC.

Open day at Dinting on 23 October 1975 saw visitors being given footplate rides on the 1923-vintage saddle tank on the left. Preserved Jubilee Class No.5690 *Leander* can be seen in the background while the strange-looking machine on the right is a diesel *RS8* that started out as a steam locomotive. During 1960, the ICI South Central Workshops at Tunstead cobbled *RS8* together out of a diesel-hydraulic engine supplied by Rolls-Royce and the frames of an Avonside Engine Co 0-4-0ST, originally built in 1923.

Thirty years on and *RS8* was to be found standing somewhat worse for wear on an isolated track panel in the car park at the National Stone Centre near Wirksworth. The National Stone Centre is only a few hundred metres from the Steeple Grange Light Railway.

In May 1978 BR confirmed that from the following June it would be directly sponsoring a series of steam-hauled rail tours for the first time since 1968. The Eastern Region confirmed that on Sundays between 25 June and 3 September it would operate a York circular via Knaresborough, Harrogate, Leeds and Church Fenton. The trains would be hauled by either 9F 2-10-0 No.92220 *Evening Star*, the last steam locomotive to be built for British Railways, or LNER V2 2-6-2 No.4771 *Green Arrow*. The London Midland Region would be operating the Cumbrian Coast Express on Tuesdays commencing 27 June through to the 29 August. The tour would start, diesel-hauled, from Blackpool at l0.05hrs, with steam traction taking over at Carnforth for the round trip to Ravenglass, Seascale and Sellafield. The locomotives pencilled in for these trains were the legendary LNER Pacifics *Flying Scotsman* and *Sir Nigel Gresley*. At the same time as this welcome news was appearing in the railway press, readers were expressing their concerns over the deteriorating condition of the LNER A4 *Bittern* and the BR-built A2 *Blue Peter* both of which were languishing in a shed at Walton Colliery near Wakefield with little or no sign of any work being done on them. The following month a letter from Biddy Baxter, editor of the BBC children's programme, was published in *The Railway Magazine*. Responding to readers' letters, Biddy pointed out that though the programme and the locomotive shared the same name there was no other involvement. The BBC was not involved in the engine's ownership nor had the A2 been restored with funds generated from a programme appeal. Over the summer an agreement was concluded with A2's owner which saw the engine transferred to the Dinting Railway Centre where she was photographed on 31 October.

A2 Pacific *Blue Peter* in action.

Though already under threat of closure, the Woodhead route suffered the first of three incidents in the space of four months on 10 March 1981 when an Arpley–Tinsley freight derailed as it was approaching Dinting Station, bringing down the overhead wires and causing considerable damage to the 'Up' line and 'Up' platform. Freight trains were able to start running later the same day following the introduction of a single-line working over the 'Down' between Hadfield and Dinting. Passengers weren't so lucky and had to suffer replacement buses until a diesel multiple unit service was introduced a couple of days later.

Disaster struck again on 8 April when at 02.45hrs, the Barton–Immingham anhydrous ammonia train hauled by electric locomotives Nos.76025 and 76027 derailed on a crossover at the west end of Hadfield Station. Our picture clearly shows the band round the waist of the tanks denoting hazardous contents and as a precaution 30 nearby houses were evacuated.

Ironically freight trains had only been using this crossover since the previous incident, as rather than spend money, BR had simply singled the track on the Hadfield–Dinting section.

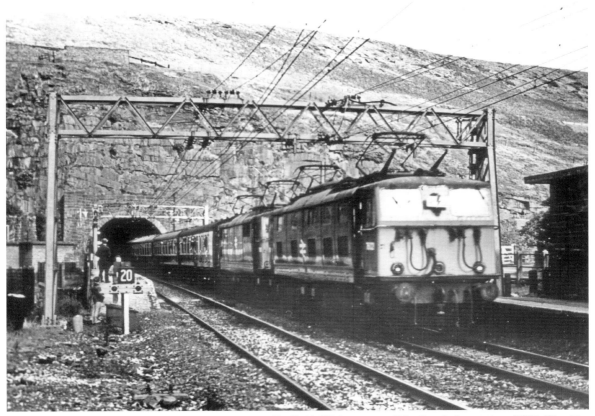

Built specifically to handle freight on the Manchester–Sheffield–Wath route via Woodhead, the origins of BR's Class76 Bo+Bo electric locomotives goes back to the days of the LNER. Electrification of the Woodhead route had been considered as early as 1926, but it wasn't until 1938 that work commenced. Under the direction of Sir Nigel Gresley a prototype Bo+Bo locomotive No.6701 – the Bo+Bo signifying that its bogies were articulated – was completed at Doncaster Works in 1941. However, by then the outbreak of war meant the cancellation of electrification work for the duration. No.6701 spent much of its time idle apart from a few test runs on existing LNER 1500V DC lines.

In June 1946 the locomotive was renumbered No.6000. By this time, work had also resumed, but progress was slow and completion of the project was expected to be delayed even further following the decision to bore a new double-line tunnel at Woodhead instead of using the old Great Central single bore tunnels. In the meantime No.6000 had been loaned to the Netherlands State Railways which was suffering a severe motive power shortage. By the time it returned home in 1952 the locomotive had had 20000 added to its number by BR. It was also sporting the name *Tommy* – the nickname given to British soldiers during both world wars and given to it by Dutch railwaymen – which it would carry throughout its career. Lessons learned from Tommy's service in the Netherlands resulted in modifications to its 56 classmates which were built by BR at Gorton. Readers might remember the Virgin Trains ads of 2007 which claimed that their electric trains 'returned power to the national grid' when braking. Well over 50 years earlier the EM1s were also doing it. Regenerative braking as it is called converts some of the kinetic energy into electricity; the motors in effect act like dynamos and generate power. The electricity generated is then fed back into the overhead wires. Locomotives applying their brakes on the down gradients either side of Woodhead Tunnel returned electricity to the overheads, thereby helping to power locomotives travelling up hill.

Our picture shows two Class76s – formerly known as EM1s – hauling an enthusiasts' rail tour over the route just a few weeks before it was closed to traffic.

Woodhead Station at the
western end of Woodhead
Tunnel on 18 December 1963.

Woodhead in the snow on
9 April 1983.

This commanding view of
Woodhead Station dates
from 18 December 1963.
In the distance a
Sheffield-bound freight
train stands in the loop,
enabling a faster service to
pass it.

THE HOPE VALLEY TO CHESTERFIELD

Preserved Jubilee Class
4-6-0 No.5596 *Bahamas*
at Edale in 1973.

This is Hope at the beginning of June 1958, shortly after the announcement that it had been voted best-kept station in the Rotherham area; an improvement on the previous year when it had taken second place. The superb display of blooms was down to the efforts of the station's gardening team comprising stationmaster P. H. Smith; porters Grassby and Oakes, and junior porters Bramwell and Knowles. Shortly afterwards the gardens were wrecked by hooligans.

Hope Station on 23 March 1963.

Clearing up operations are underway
following the derailment of a mail train at
Hope in May 1983.

Hasland-based 8F 2-8-0 No.48371 trundles through Bamford Rotherham Operating District on 4 October 1956, as the aptly-named stationmaster Mr F. Bamford and a porter admire what is left of the blooms that helped them win the Special Class Prize and Shield in the annual Rotherham Operating District station gardens competition.

When this picture of Hathersage Station was taken on 11 September 1969, the place had been reduced to a sorry state thanks to de-staffing and the introduction of Pay Trains.

EASTER RAIL CRUISE IN DERBYSHIRE

CHEAP TRIP

BY

DIESEL TRAIN

HATHERSAGE

Sunday 14th April 1963

FROM	TIMES OF DEPARTURE	RETURN FARES Second Class	ARRIVAL TIMES ON RETURN
	pm	s d	pm
NOTTINGHAM Midland	2 30	8/2	8 43
BEESTON...	2 38		8 34
TRENT	2 45		8 24
SAWLEY JUNCTION	2 50		8 18
DRAYCOTT & BREASTON	2 55	7/6	8 14
BORROWASH	3 1		8 8
SPONDON	3 5		8 4
DERBY Midland	3 15	7/3	7 55
BELPER	3 29	5/6	7 43
AMBERGATE	3 35	5/3	7 36
	pm	Passengers return	pm
HATHERSAGE ... arrive	5 20	same day at ...	6 55

The train will proceed on the outward journey through the beautiful Derbyshire dales via Matlock, Bakewell and Miller's Dale and thence through the Hope Valley to Hathersage allowing approximately 1½ hours' stay at that point. The return journey will be made via Grindleford, Chesterfield and Wingfield.

Children under 3 years of age, free; 3 years and under 14, half-fares (fractions of a 1d. reckoned as a 1d.).

Rail tickets can be obtained in advance at stations and official railway agents

Further information will be supplied on application to stations, official railway agents, or to Commercial Manager, Alan House, Clumber Street, Nottingham. Telephone 48531, Extn. 40.

LONDON MIDLAND   Travel In Rail Comfort   March 1963   BR 35000

Arthur Gover & Sons (Printers) Ltd, Heanor, Derbyshire

This picture of Hathersage was taken on 26 March 1963 for a feature on local stations threatened with closure. The Beeching Plan was advocating that there should be only one direct route between Manchester and Sheffield and that it should be the electrified one via Woodhead and Penistone. As it was, local opposition along the Hope Valley was such that eventually the Woodhead route was axed instead.

This picture of Grindleford looking toward Hathersage is another of those taken on 26 March 1963 for a feature on local stations threatened with closure.

Grindleford station on 5 August 1994.

Track maintenance and renewals along the Hope Valley line during November 2007 resulted in the former goods yard at Grindleford being used to prepare machines in readiness for working during the night. A Network Rail Jackson stoneblower is being readied while behind stands a Road-Rail vehicle.

The date is 31 August 1939 and as Europe drifted inexorably to war, Northern Command militia units were to be found already guarding strategic locations such as Totley Tunnel – at 3 miles 950yards, Britain's second longest tunnel – against possible sabotage.

The tunnel was blocked on 24 May 1971, when a nine-coach Manchester Piccadilly to London St Pancras service derailed at 50mph about one mile from the western portal. Though the entire train came off the track, none of the 25 passengers on board was seriously injured. A rescue diesel multiple unit was launched from Manchester but could not get close enough because of debris. A second attempt was made from the Sheffield end and the passengers were evacuated to Chesterfield. It took three days to clear the line and return it to normal working.

On 21 June 1966 a freight train hauled by English Electric Type3 D6863 smashed into the rear of another goods train near Dore West signal box blocking the Hope Valley line between Sheffield and Chinley for about 36 hours.

This is the Midland Railway mileage chart for Dore & Totley Station and the junctions linking the Chesterfield and Sheffield with the Hope Valley line.

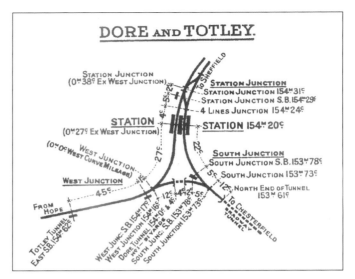

In January 1964 one of our photographers was invited along to Bradway Tunnel to photograph repair work being carried out to a section of the roof. For years the tunnel had suffered from the effects of water seepage causing sections of the brick lining to bulge.

Workers pack the roof with wooden supports.

This close-up gives us some idea of the state of some sections of the brick lining at the time. Following the 1990s rail privatisation, Railtrack undertook a major maintenance project on the tunnel as part of the upgrading of the Midland Main Line network. This involved replacing the bulged areas of brickwork completely, but to do this a temporary support system had to be installed to maintain the integrity of the rest of the tunnel lining. The main contractor, Amalgamated Construction, called in Weldgrip Geotechnical who used their high-density rockbolts and a polymer geogrid to create a support system that would allow the bulged area to be cut out and replaced.

Landslips are surprisingly common on Britain's railway network, the majority occurring after periods of heavy rain. This particular one at the southern end of the 2,027-yards-long Bradway Tunnel, just one mile north of Dronfield, occurred in January 1990.

This is what Dronfield Station looked like during the early years of the 20th century.

This is Dronfield Station – or rather what was left of it – on 25 July 1979, when our photographer visited for a story on it reopening to passengers. BR had originally closed it to passengers on 2 January 1967, though it remained open for goods traffic for a few months more before shutting completely.

Members of Derbyshire County Council and North East Derbyshire District Council, along with representatives from BR, visited Dronfield on 8 October 1980 to view progress and improvements being earned out in readiness for the station's reopening.

A south-bound express attracts the attention of some of the councillors as it thunders through Dronfield.

It must have seemed as though the whole of Dronfield had turned out to watch – or catch –the first train to Sheffield on the morning of their station's re-opening on 5 January 1981.

BR engineers put the finishing touches to their preparations to blow the 'lid' off Broomhouse Tunnel and turn it into a cutting. The line was closed on 17 August and the roof was blown off with explosives two days later. North-bound trains were diverted via Barrow Hill, Beighton Junction and Rotherham Masboro', and freight was sent via Kirkby and Mansfield.

September 1969 and trains are once again running on the Chesterfield–Sheffield main line at Sheepbridge after the removal of the 88-yard-long Broomhouse Tunnel. As can be seen here, the old sign at what used to be the entrance to the tunnel was left in place.

Sheepbridge Ironworks and sidings in 1939.

0-4-0ST *DNT* was built for the Staveley Iron Company in 1949 by commercial locomotive builders William Bagnall & Co of Stafford. The angular saddle tank was unusual for locomotives built by this firm. (Vic Hall)

There is confusion in some quarters over these pictures, which were originally published as postcards, as it was thought they showed the clearing up operations following an accident at Tapton Junction in 1919. However as one of them carries a 1906 postmark, the accident is in fact the wreck of the "Paddy Mail", which made front page news in the *Derbyshire Times* on 15 September 1906; the incident having occurred three days earlier.

"The Paddy Mail" – the familiar name in colliery districts for the workmen's train – is almost a household word in an area like Chesterfield. Every day, morning and night, hundreds – indeed thousands – of men who work underground are conveyed to and from their work over distances ranging from two to perhaps ten miles. Knowing this, as the residents of Chesterfield district do, a natural dread descended upon Chesterfield and district that Tuesday morning, when the news went round that the Grassmoor "mail" on the Midland Railway had met with disaster near Tapton. Early as it was, many people crowded towards the railway bridge on the Brimington Road from which they could view the site of the collision.

The miners' train on its way to Grassmoor had run into a light engine which was standing on the up main line. The tenders of both locomotives had been wrecked by the collision, and one coach of the train had been hopelessly shattered, while all the others suffered sufficient damage to render them useless as rolling stock. The fact that a large number of miners were travelling on the train gave rise to a needless alarm as to the extent of the injuries suffered by the workmen, but fortunately this proved groundless, although it was only by the greatest good fortune that the accident was not attended by loss of life. Probably the greater proportion of the 200 men on board were injured in some manner, but those who were able to went straight home, allowing the doctors and ambulance men, who were early on the scene, to concentrate their attention on the men requiring the most careful treatment.

The train to which the mishap occurred was transporting the miners from Dronfield, Unstone, Sheepbridge and Chesterfield to the Grassmoor Collieries, with some of the men joining the Glapwell "mail" at Chesterfield. At the same time, an engine had arrived at Tapton Junction from Staveley, with the object of taking out a ballast train which stood in its own siding on the west side of the main lines. From Staveley it arrived on the goods line and in order to reach the ballast siding, it had to cross over the main passenger lines. The driver, Sam Machin, and the fireman, Dixon, of Staveley, in making the move, got over the down passenger line but found the "dummy" - as the signal there is called - against them, and so remained with the engine on the up line, almost under the bridge which carries the Chesterfield and Brimington road over the railway. Thus, the ballast engine stood right in the track of the "mail" for which the signals were clear.

Although it was travelling at a relatively slow speed due to heavy fog, the driver on the workmen's train, Joe Williams, heard no fog detonator and so proceeded on his way, quite unaware of the presence of the locomotive near the bridge into which the tender of his engine, which was travelling backwards, then crashed. The force of the collision derailed both engines and the first coach of the twelve comprising the workmen's train. A sudden stop, and then the "mail" engine again scraped forward dragging the derailed coach with it. The weight of the other carriages on the first carriage caused it to rear up against the engine, and the sight of its wheels over the funnel of the locomotive met those who first arrived on the scene.

At the Tapton Junction signal box, the man on duty, named Warren, was a temporary signalman, due to finish his shift at 6am. He had "pegged off" (as the railway men say) the light engine to allow it to get as far up the line as possible, but had not altered the final signal to allow it to go into the siding. On the other hand the signals were clear for the "Paddy Mail" – perhaps this was due to the signalman hoping to get the "mail" through in plenty of time before the Scotch express was due to pass, causing him to forget the ballast engine – and the workmen's train was allowed to come on without any warning of the obstruction. The regular signalman, Jones, came on duty at six o'clock, a few minutes after the mishap.

Preserved Midland Railway three-cylinder compound 4-4-0 No.1000 sprints through Tapton at the head of a Stephenson Locomotive Society special on 30 August 1959.

The Midland Railway station at Chesterfield; pictured here in 1888, opened for traffic on 2 May 1870, replacing the earlier rather elegant but no longer practical station designed by Francis Thompson for the North Midland Railway.

Staff at the Midland Station. Note the wooden platforms. Prior to 1907 there were three stations in the town all called Chesterfield, and the only reason there was a change was due to the Great Central's acquisition of the Lancashire, Derbyshire & Lincolnshire Railway. As they now owned two stations with the same name, confusion was avoided by renaming one Chesterfield Market Place, and the other, Chesterfield Central. The Midland station was known as Chesterfield until September 1950 when for a few months it became Chesterfield St Mary's. In June 1951 it was renamed Chesterfield Midland, but reverted back to Chesterfield in 1964 by which time the other two had closed.

This picture of the Midland Station dates from 1908 and was originally published as a postcard by W.H.Smith. (Chesterfield Local Studies Library)

A hundred years separates this picture from the previous one. In that time the station has been transformed, though the original canopy supports have survived. (Clive Hardy)

Photographer Harry Townley took this picture of Stanier Black 5 4-6-0 No.44828 rolling into Chesterfield Midland at the head of a Derby-bound train. (C.M. & J.M.Bentley)

It was only a few weeks after the end of steam traction on British Railways – apart from the narrow gauge Vale of Rheidol line – yet hundreds of people turned out to see *Flying Scotsman* take out a special train. At the time *Flying Scotsman* was the only steam locomotive allowed on the national network as its owner had a contractual agreement with BR until 1971.

Designed by Derbyshire-born Sir Nigel Gresley for the Great Northern Railway, construction of Al Class Pacific No.1472 began at Doncaster Works during the latter months of 1922. However, by the time the locomotive was completed at a cost of £7,944, the GNR no longer existed as an independent company; it had been absorbed into the newly created London & North Eastern Railway so the as yet unnamed No.1472 left the Works in LNER livery.

That this engine was chosen to represent the LNER at the 1924 British Empire Exhibition is something of a fluke. In December 1923, No.1472 was in Doncaster Works to have its centre piston rod replaced but there were no spares available. As the exhibition locomotive was going to be out of action for the best part of a year, why lose the services of an operational machine when here was one that was inoperable? Thus No.1472 was given a cosmetic overhaul, brass adornment and a repaint, which included having the LNER coat of arms painted on her cab sides and then polished again and again and again until she sparkled. Also former GNR locomotives had 3,000 added to their numbers so No.1472 became No.4472. Knowing the value of publicity, the LNER decided to name her *Flying Scotsman*. The choice was nothing short of inspirational as the name was already well-known to the well-heeled travelling public as the Flying Scotsman train which ran between Kings Cross and Edinburgh – the country's most famous passenger service.

On 1 May 1928 *Flying Scotsman* was assured a place in British railway history when she hauled the LNER's first non-stop London–Edinburgh express; a run of nearly 400 miles. Forty years later on 1 May 1968, *Flying Scotsman* departed Kings Cross at l0.00hrs on the dot hauling a non-stop anniversary special. Simultaneously the regular Flying Scotsman service departed from platform 8 hauled by Deltic No.D9021 *Argyll & Sutherland Highlander*.

Enthusiasts turned out to watch preserved LNER 4-6-2 *Flying Scotsman* steam through Chesterfield on its way to Derby Works for an overhaul following its return from the United States.

With the Beeching Axe in full swing it was pleasing to know that a handful of stations were being modernised – including Chesterfield Midland.

College of Art students Belinda Smith (left) and Ruth Paling pictured at the unveiling of their waiting room murals at Chesterfield Midland. Also in the picture is BR Area Manager David Knight.

Chesterfield station was extensively rebuilt shortly after Midland Mainline took over from BR. At present the station has only two platforms, the old bays of earlier years no longer exist though there is a proposal to build an additional platform adjacent to the Down slow goods line as part of the East Midlands North Erewash re-signalling scheme. This line is signalled for bi-directional working and the new Chesterfield South Junction to Tapton Junction layout would enable passenger services to continue using the station during engineering blockades on the fast lines. The station is now served by East Midland Trains and Cross Country. The picture was taken on a grey day in November 2007.

This imposing statue of railway pioneer and first president of the Institute of Mechanical Engineers, George Stephenson, was erected outside Chesterfield station in 2004. In 1838 he bought nearby Tapton House and it remained his home until his death ten years later. (Clive Hardy)

In November 1996 Richard Branson's Virgin Group outbid its rivals to take over the 1,500 mile franchise, created out of what had been British Rail's Cross Country services. In return for a 15-year deal, instead of the regular 7-year franchise, Virgin undertook not only to turn what had been a loss-making sub-sector of BR's InterCity Division into a profitable operation, but to pay a £10 million premium by the end of the franchise. Cross Country had always been something of a ragbag outfit, having to rely on locomotives and rolling stock being cascaded down to it rather than receiving new-build equipment. And it never broke even, running up losses of £128 million in its last year under BR control.

Virgin Cross Country took over services from BR on 5 January 1997. During December 1998 a £1.6 billion financing arrangement meant Virgin could expect to take delivery of the first of 78 new *Voyager* 125mph air-conditioned diesel-electric multiple units from Bombardier Transportation by the end of 2000. As well as air-conditioning, each unit had decent toilets, a shop, and 'at-seat' audio entertainment. The *Voyagers* were noted for their smooth running and rapid acceleration, essential if Virgin was to stick to its proposed new timetable which, when introduced, would cut journey times by no less than 20 per cent.

At first the *Voyagers* proved unpopular with much of the travelling public. The seats were too narrow, there was hardly any luggage space, and for many passengers the experience of travelling in one of these units when it was overcrowded was akin to being in a tin of sardines. This was partially remedied with the removal of some seats to create luggage space, while the Strategic Rail Authority instructed other train operating companies to provide additional services for commuters, for example, between Chesterfield and Sheffield, in order to ease the overcrowding. With Bombardier delivering *Voyager* sets at the rate of one a week, Virgin was in the position to go live with its new timetable from 30 September 2002, with over 60 sets scheduled to work every weekday.

The Achilles heel of the new timetable was Birmingham New Street Station, the hub of the cross country network, very busy, very noisy, congested at the best of times and easily thrown into chaos. For Virgin's timetable to stand any chance of success the trains belonging to other franchises using New Street had to run on time. Most of the time they didn't and Virgin had little alternative than to make amendments.

Our pictures were taken in November 2008, the very month Virgin Cross Country announced record passenger figures of 24 million, and the very month the franchise was taken over by Arriva. Virgin had always found the going tough, struggling to reach financial targets and in 2003 the Group was allowed to transfer some services from its Cross Country to its West Coast franchise which was in effect a separate train operating company. Virgin was allowed to renegotiate the terms of its Cross Country business which effectively guaranteed a profit, and the franchise would be terminated in 2008 instead of 2012.

The revised franchise was put out to tender during 2007, with Virgin locking horns with three other contenders; Arriva, First Group and National Express. On 10 July the Strategic Rail Authority's successor, the Department for Transport, announced that Arriva had secured the franchise, to be known as New Cross Country, which would operate from 11 November 2007 to 11 March 2016. Arriva is believed to be planning to remove the shop and one toilet from each *Voyager* to provide much needed additional luggage space. Other alterations include free wi-fi for passengers, at-seat catering, and at-home printing of tickets.

Between 1 January and 24 August 1932, the LMS set about replacing Horn's Bridge at a cost in excess of £30,000. (Chesterfield Local Studies Library)

The Mayor of Chesterfield, Alderman T. D. Sims, performs the official opening of the new Horn's Bridge on 24 August 1932. (Chesterfield Local Studies Library)

The last operational 2-6-2+2-6-2T Beyer-Garratt articulated locomotive on British Railways was Hasland-based No.47994. She made her last revenue earning run on Friday 28 February 1958, hauling a mineral train from Toton to Hasland prior to departing for Crewe Works on Friday 14 March. She was officially withdrawn from service on 29 March. (F.Elliot)

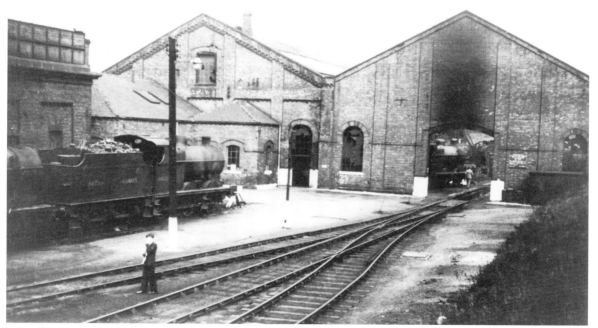

When Hasland roundhouse near Chesterfield was opened by the Midland Railway in 1875 it had a slated roof, but at some stage it was re-clad in corrugated iron. Our picture shows the south end of the facility; locomotives can be seen stabled inside round the turntable. Eventually part of the roof had to be taken down for safety reasons as mining subsidence was affecting the fabric of the building. The depot closed during 1964. (Chesterfield Local Studies Library)

Born out of wartime necessity the 'Austerity' 0-6-0 saddle tank (0-6-0ST) turned out to be one of the most successful designs for a shunting engine ever produced in the UK. The design team, led by the Deputy Director of RE Equipment, R. A. Riddles, took as their starting point an existing industrial shunting engine design – the Hunslet Engine Co's inside cylinder 0-6-0ST –modifying it to meet Ministry of Supply specifications. To save time, money and materials, cast-iron was used where possible, and, taking a leaf out of the Victory ship building programme, welded assemblies were used wherever practical such as the cab and coal bunker; the saddle water tank, and the main frames. Another modification on the original design was the extension of the saddle tank over the smokebox.

Nearly 400 of these engines were ordered by the Ministry of Supply, their construction split between a number of commercial manufacturers including the Hunslet Engine Co; Hudswell, Clarke & Co; Robert Stephenson & Hawthorn; Andrew Barclay & Co, and William Bagnall & Co. The design proved powerful and robust, and in 1946 the LNER purchased 75 of them from the War Department. The LNER 'Austerities' were designated Class J94, the 'J' prefix identifying them as having the 0-6-0 wheel arrangement (in fact the LNER applied a letter prefix to all their locomotives classes: a 4-6-2 wheel arrangement had the prefix 'A'; all classes with a 4-6-0 wheel arrangement were prefixed 'B', and so on).

On nationalisation the J94s were given BR numbers 68006–68080, and on 10 August 1956, No.68030 was trialled on the Cromford & High Peak line to assess whether or not the class would make suitable replacements for four ageing tank engines built in the 19th century by the old North London Railway. By the end of 1957, three more J94s were resident on the C&HP: Nos.68006, 68013 and 68034, and by the time the line closed, 68012, 68068 and 68079 had also seen service on it.

This is the spar washer at Fallgate on the ALR.

Remnants of the narrow gauge Ashover Light Railway
were still in evidence when this picture was taken on 1
March 1971. Here a set of points is still in situ on the
stone bridge over the River Amber at Butts Quarry.
When the railway was first proposed this quarry was still
being worked by hand and employed just two men who
would break the stone by hand. One of the main reasons
for building the ALR is that it would enable output
from this quarry to be vastly increased and it was
anticipated that the workforce would increase to
between 60 and 70 men. When Butts Quarry closed on
28 January 1950, it wasn't because it was worked out –
BR had cancelled its standing order for ballast, thus
making the place uneconomical to keep open.

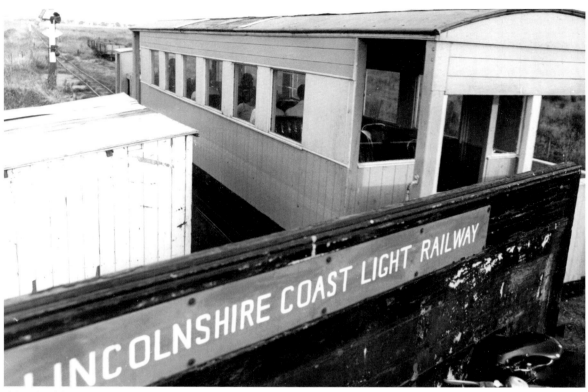

After the ALR ceased operations, its passenger coaches were locked away and there they remained until the new sports field at Clay Cross opened in the early 1950s. Someone had the idea that perhaps the old coaches could be utilised and four of them were dragged out; one positioned by the bowling green, the rest by the football pitch. All were modified having bits either boarded over, removed, or both, and the old longitudinal seats were removed with spectators parking their bottoms on fold-up chairs instead.

In around 1960, the Lincolnshire Coast Light Railway, a narrow gauge line operating at Humberston near Cleethorpes, bought the remains of two of these coaches and set about rebuilding them. The bodies were mounted on old bogie wagon bogies with seats salvaged from scrapped Glasgow tramcars. One of the carriages entered service in April 1962, the other in November 1963.

THE ASHOVER LIGHT RAILWAY.

TIME TABLE.　　From JUNE 6th, 1936, until further notice.
ON WEDNESDAYS, SATURDAYS and SUNDAYS ONLY.

UP TRAINS.	WEDNESDAYS & SATURDAYS ONLY.						SUNDAY			DOWN TRAINS.	WEDNESDAYS & SATURDAYS ONLY.						SUNDAY		
	a.m.	a.m.	p.m.	p.m.	p.m.	p.m.	p.m.	p.m.	p.m.		a.m.	a.m.	p.m.	p.m.	p.m.	p.m.	p.m.	p.m.	p.m.
CLAY CROSS and EGSTOW dep.	7 40	9 55	12 18	2 45	4 40	7 0	2 45	6 0	7 10	Ashover (Butts) dep.	8 32	11 0	1 30	3 45	6 0	8 15	3 45	5 10	8 30
CHESTERFIELD ROAD ,,	7 42	9 57	12 17	2 47	4 59	7 2	2 47	6 2	7 12	Salter Lane (H) ,,	8 35	11 2	1 32	3 47	6 2	8 17	3 47	5 12	8 32
Holmgate (H) ,,	7 46	10 5	12 22	2 55	5 0	7 10	2 52	6 7	7 17	Fallgate	8 41	11 8	1 88	3 53	6 8	8 23	3 53	5 18	8 38
Springfield (H) ,,	7 49	10 6	12 24	2 55	5 1	7 11	2 53	6 8	7 18	Milltown (H) ,,	8 44	11 11	1 41	3 56	6 11	8 26	3 56	5 21	8 41
Clay Lane (H) ,,	7 50	10 7	12 27	2 57	5 3	7 12	2 54	6 9	7 19	Woolley ,,	8 51	11 17	1 47	4 2	6 17	8 32	4 2	5 27	8 47
STRETTON ,,	7 55	10 14	12 32	3 2	5 7	7 17	2 59	5 14	7 21	STRETTON ,,	8 55	11 19	1 49	4 4	6 19	8 34	4 4	5 29	8 49
Hurst Lane (H) ,,	8 5	10 24	12 42	3 12	5 17	7 27	3 9	5 24	7 34	Hurst Lane (H) ,,	9 5	11 28	1 54	4 18	6 28	8 43	4 18	5 38	8 58
Woolley ,,	8 8	10 27	12 45	3 15	5 20	7 30	3 12	5 27	7 37	Clay Lane (H) ,,	9 18	11 34	2 4	4 29	6 34	8 55	4 28	5 48	9 6
Dale Bank (H) ,,	8 11	10 30	12 48	3 18	5 33	7 33	3 15	5 30	7 40	Springfield (H) ,,	9 18	11 41	2 11	4 26	6 41	8 56	4 26	5 51	9 11
Milltown (H) ,,	8 14	10 33	12 51	3 31	5 36	7 36	3 18	5 33	7 43	Holmgate (H) ,,	9 28	11 48	2 18	4 28	6 48	8 58	4 28	5 58	9 13
FALLGATE ,,	8 21	10 40	12 58	3 28	5 38	7 39	3 25	5 40	7 46	CHESTERFIELD ROAD ,,	9 30	11 50	2 20	4 35	6 50	9 2	4 35	7 0	9 17
Salter Lane (H) ,,	8 34	10 43	1 1	3 31	5 36	7 42	3 28	5 43	7 53	CLAY CROSS and EGSTOW arr.	9 35	11 55	2 23	4 40	6 55	9 5	4 40	7 5	9 20
Ashover (Butts) arr.	8 37	10 45	1 4	3 34	5 39	7 45	3 31	5 45	8 0										

Note :— (H) denotes that the Trains will only stop at these Halts when required to set down passengers & pick up passengers by request.
Passengers joining trains at the Halts should be there five minutes before the time shown in time-table.

CHEAP RETURN TICKETS

CLAY CROSS, any station, and STRETTON, 6d. return.
:: Single Journey Fares at Ordinary Rates. ::

Jos. Spriggs & Sons, General Printers, Clay Cross.

G. H. WILBRAHAM, Manager.

Clay Cross No.4 Pit forms the backdrop to this picture of local miners waiting to board at the Midland Railway Station for their annual Territorial Army summer camp. This postcard is number 110 in a series published by the Clay Cross Company. They were often used by the company to acknowledge letters, the payment of invoices, enquiries and so on. (Chesterfield Local Studies Library)

This Clay Cross Co. tub – one of a number still on site in March 1971 – would not have been hauled by one of the ALR's locomotives; it would have been pushed along by a couple of workers.

This postcard published by the Clay Cross Co. shows a couple of loaded tubs being pushed into the lift for hauling to the surface. (Chesterfield Local Studies Library)

EAST OF CHESTERFIELD

This picture of the Manchester, Sheffield & Lincolnshire Railway Station at Chesterfield was taken some time after 1897 following the company's change of name to the Great Central. (Chesterfield Local Studies Library)

Taken from Wharf Lane footbridge, which straddled the station throat at Chesterfield Central, this picture probably dates from the late 1950s. The large building on the left is the goods warehouse which at this time still had a line running through it, allowing wagons and vans to be loaded and unloaded inside the building. By 1961 this had been removed and the entrance bricked up. The building was still used though loading and unloading was done through three of the windows which were knocked through for the purpose. These can be identified in later pictures as they have corrugated iron hoods over them.

In the background, the locomotive belching out steam has just crossed over from the 'Down' main – the ground signal is still showing off – with a terminating train from Nottingham Victoria and is in the process of propelling it out of the way and into the siding behind the 'Up' platform. Despite appearances in photographs, the 'Up' platform for trains in the direction of Heath Junction, Annesley and Nottingham Victoria was always one-sided. It was impossible for passengers to board a train that was standing on the siding as there was a fence in the way.

GWR-trained John G. Robinson joined the Great Central Railway as Locomotive Engineer in 1900, having previously been in charge of the Locomotive, Carriage & Wagon Department of the Waterford, Limerick & Western Railway. One of his locomotive designs for the GCR was these 4-6-2 tank engines, built specifically to handle heavy suburban trains in and out of Marylebone. Designated Class 9N by the GCR, they were among the first locomotives owned by the railway to be equipped with superheaters.

Between 1911 and 1926, 44 of these sturdy engines were built in a total of five batches; three by the GCR themselves; one by the LNER; and the last by commercial locomotive builders Hawthorn, Leslie & Co. (Chesterfield Local Studies Library)

One of the most iconic railway posters of all time is John Hassell's 'Jolly Fisherman' which he painted for the LNER in 1923, though he had produced an almost identical one for the Great Northern Railway in 1908. His original 31x23inch artwork was discovered in a garden shed in Hornchurch, Essex, in 1995 and was later auctioned at Onslow's.

Had the Lancashire, Derbyshire & East Coast Railway been built as originally planned its main line would have extended from the Manchester Ship Canal near Warrington and then by way of Knutsford, Prestbury, Chesterfield and Lincoln, to Busby on the Sutton–Willoughby line a total distance in excess of 130 miles. The plan also envisaged the company's headquarters being situated at Macclesfield. With the abandonment of the full coast-to-coast scheme and all works west of Chesterfield, the latter became the obvious choice for the company's headquarters, which were eventually housed in the splendid Jacobean-style station situated in West Bars. Better known as Chesterfield Market Place, this station closed to passengers on 3 December 1951 and to goods traffic on 4 March 1957.

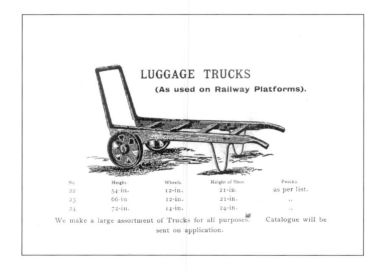

LUGGAGE TRUCKS
(As used on Railway Platforms).

No	Height	Wheels.	Height of Shoe	PRICES.
22	54-in.	12-in.	21-in.	as per list.
23	66-in	12-in.	21-in.	,,
24	72-in.	14-in.	24-in.	,,

We make a large assortment of Trucks for all purposes. Catalogue will be sent on application.

Chesterfield Market Place Station after the Second World War and shortly before nationalisation. The station had four platforms No's. 1, 2, 4 and 5. There was no platform 3 as the numbering appears to have followed the American or European practice of allocating numbers to tracks; track 3 was the engine release road for platforms 2 and 4. (G. Perrin courtesy of Chesterfield Local Studies Library)

Chesterfield Market Place Station in 1948. When British Railways came into existence on 1 January 1948, overnight it became the country's biggest single employer, with a mind-blowing inventory of 52,000 miles of track; 20,000+ locomotives, over one million assorted freight vehicles and 41,000 passenger carriages. That wasn't all. It also owned 70 hotels, 50,000 railway houses and 100 steamships. Also, there

were thousands of motor vehicles ranging from cars to heavy lorries, as well as around 8,000 horses and well over 20,000 horse-drawn carts.

This picture of Chesterfield Market Place Station was taken in February 1973 to accompany publication of the news that it was to be demolished to make way for a new road.

A LD&ECR passenger tank engine works hard as it hauls its train across Chesterfield Viaduct a massive 700-foot-long structure that carried the company's tracks over the River Hipper and the Midland and Great Central railway lines. The Midland line is the one with the coal train disappearing off to the left; the Great Central's Chesterfield Loop Line is at the bottom of the pile.

The LD&ECR were more interested in running coal trains than passenger traffic, and why not as few companies made money carrying passengers. In fact when the line opened for business the LD&ECR didn't have any passenger carriages of its own and relied on some old Great Eastern Railway six-wheelers that it had managed to get its hands on. Temporary passenger services commenced in December 1896, with the full main line weekday timetable of four trains each way began the following March. For those in search of a night out, the railway also ran a 22.00hrs Saturdays-only 'all stations Chesterfield–Warsop' service, though missing it could present the errant traveller with a few problems as there was no Sunday service. (Chesterfield Local Studies Library)

The last remnant of Chesterfield Viaduct was demolished in late 1984 to make way for road improvements around the town.

In a previous existence LNER 0-6-4T No.6153 was one of six Class D engines built for the Lancashire, Derbyshire & East Coast Railway in 1904 by Kitson & Co. of Leeds. They were the first new locomotives ordered by the LD&ECR in four years and this one, their No.34, was the last to be owned by the company prior to it being taken over by the Great Central Railway. Based at Tuxford, they were also the most powerful locomotives on the LD&ECR roster, their 3,000gallon capacity water tanks and a coal bunker capable of holding four tons enabled them to haul non-stop long-distance coal trains to Grimsby. So successful were they that the LD&ECR ordered three additional engines from Kitsons which were delivered in December 1906, just a couple of weeks prior to the Great Central taking over. It is said that they were delivered already painted in GCR livery carrying numbers 1145–1147, but in order to stick to the official niceties the GCR referred to them as engines A1–A3 in written documents.

During 1899 the LD&ECR was losing business due to a shortage of coal trucks which it sought to rectify through a combination of buying, hiring and leasing vehicles. This pattern continued up to the railway's takeover by the Great Central. In 1902, for example, 215 wagons were hired from W.H.Davis who had a depot at Langwith Junction, and a further 265 wagons were leased from the Ince Waggon & Ironworks Co. of Wigan. Between 1900 and 1913, output from the Yorkshire coalfields rose from 28,250,679 to 43,680,016 tons. During the same period the combined output of the Derbyshire, Notts and Leicestershire coalfields increased from 25,977,987 to 33,702,521 tons.

Scarcliffe on the LD&ECR line to Langwith Junction had a weekday service of just four trains each-way when this picture of the stationmaster and his family was taken in 1911.

The antics of the photographer appear to have caught the attention of the local track gang in this pre-Great War picture of Langwith Junction. Despite its size, Langwith Junction's weekday passenger services at the time were light; just four trains each-way to Chesterfield and five trains each-way to Sheffield. On 2 June 1924 the station was renamed Shirebrook North; there was also a Shirebrook South and a Shirebrook West. Shirebrook North closed to passenger traffic on 19 September 1955, though until the mid-1960s it was a picking up and setting down stop for summer holiday trains. Shirebrook South on the former Great Northern line closed to passengers on 14 September 1931; Shirebrook West on the former Midland line closed on 12 October 1964.

A53/R(5/Adex)

EASTER HOLIDAYS 1963

day trips | Sunday 14th / Monday 15th / Tuesday 16th | April

BOSTON & SKEGNESS

FROM	TIMES OF DEPARTURE				RETURN FARES Second Class to	
	*14th April	*15th April	15th April	16th April	Boston	Skegness
	am	am	am	am	s d	s d
DERBY Friargate	8 16	8 40		8 45	13/9	15/4
WEST HALLAM		9 0		8 57	13/9	14/4
ILKESTON North	8 34	9 8		9 5	13/9	14/4
AWSWORTH		9 13		9 10	12/9	14/4
KIMBERLEY		9 18		9 14	12/9	14/4
BASFORD North	8 42	9 26		9 24	11/6	13/6
SHIREBROOK North	8 50				11/6	13/6
SHIREBROOK South			9 22		13/3	14/-
PLEASLEY EAST			9 37		13/3	14/-
SUTTON-IN-ASHFIELD Town			9 35		13/3	14/-
HUCKNALL Central			9 44		12/9	13/6
NEW BASFORD			10 0		11/6	13/6
NOTTINGHAM Victoria	8 56	9 32		9 30	11/6	13/6
NETHERFIELD & COLWICK	9 5	9 42		9 40	11/6	13/6
	9 15			9 50	11/6	13/6
	am	am	am	am		
BOSTON .... arrive	NB	10 58	11 46	NB		
	am		pm			
SKEGNESS	11 9	11 42	12 28	11 44		

Passengers return same day as follows:—

		14th April	15th April	15th April	16th April
		pm	pm	pm	pm
SKEGNESS .... depart		7 1	5 50	7 34	6 44
BOSTON			6 22	8 15	
NETHERFIELD & COLWICK arrive		8 57		9 23	8 28
NOTTINGHAM Victoria		9 8	8 0	9 33	8 48
NEW BASFORD		9 18	8 9		8 56
HUCKNALL Central				9 50	
SUTTON-IN-ASHFIELD Town				10 7	
PLEASLEY East				10 16	
SHIREBROOK South				10 23	
SHIREBROOK North				(10 30)	
BASFORD North		9 24	8 15		9 3
KIMBERLEY East		9 32	8 24		9 12
AWSWORTH			8 29		9 18
ILKESTON North		9 42	8 35		9 23
WEST HALLAM			8 43		9 31
DERBY Friargate		10 0	8 57		9 44

N.B.—No bookings to BOSTON on 14th and 16th April
* Light Refreshments will be available on these trains in each direction
Children under 3 years of age, free; 3 years and under 14, half-fares (fractions of 1d. to be reckoned as 1d.)
Rail tickets can be obtained in advance at stations and official railway agents
Further information will be supplied on application to Stations, Official Railway Agents, or to
Commercial Manager, Alan House, Clumber Street, Nottingham. Telephone: Nottingham 48531, Extn. 40; or to
Traffic Manager, 26-28 Newlands, Lincoln. Telephone: Lincoln 26352
Traffic Manager, The Farm Buildings, Granville Road, Sheffield. Telephone: Sheffield 29611, Extn. 35

BRITISH RAILWAYS | March 1963 BR 35000

Arthur Gaunt & Sons (Printers) Ltd., Heanor, Derbyshire

The line between Chesterfield Market Place to Langwith Junction via Arkwright Town closed on 3 December 1951 after British Railways finally threw in the towel over problems with the notorious one mile, 864-yard-long Bolsover Tunnel which was suffering from the combined effects of mining subsidence and water seepage. The line beyond Langwith Junction to Lincoln remained open (for the time being). Langwith Junction Station, better known to many as Shirebrook North, was closed to passenger services on 19 September 1955, though summer Saturday services to the likes of Skegness continues to stop there until 5 September 1964. The station closed to goods traffic on 4 January 1965. Our pictures were taken on 11 January 1977 to illustrate a story concerning the derelict buildings and the fact that the local council wanted them demolished.

The village of Clowne was once served by two railway stations; one owned by the Midland Railway, the other by the LD&ECR. They were so close together that a siding belonging to the Midland Station can be seen on the right side of the picture of the LD&ECR station.

Former Midland Railway 1F 0-6-0T No.41734 was one of many such engines that spent part if its service at Staveley (Barrow Hill), this particular one being transferred to Birkenhead in July 1957. No fewer than 240 of these locomotives were built during the late 19th century and four of them survived almost until the end of steam on BR. That they survived at all was due to a legal agreement drawn between the old Midland Railway and the Staveley Iron Co. whereby the former would supply the latter with steam shunting engines for a period of one hundred years and by July 1966, when many modern steam engines had already been broken up, money was being raised by one of these veterans. The four were all half-cab variants; in other words their cabs didn't have a back sheet like No.41734 and were partially open to the elements.

Around £375 of the £875 needed had been raised by the 'Midland Railway 1F Tank Fund', though no decision had been taken on which engine to buy. The four were No.41708 (MR No.1418) built at Derby in 1880; No's.41763 (MR No.214) and 41804 (MR No.889) both built at Derby in 1890. And finally, No.41835 (MR No.2003) built by Vulcan Foundry, Newton-le-Willows, in 1892 and which had been re-boilered as late as 1961. At one time every weekday found Barrow Hill providing as many as five 0-6-0Ts and two 0-4-0Ts for shunting at Staveley Ironworks, and four 0-6-0Ts for shunting at Sheepbridge. To cover this work the shed had an allocation of three 0-4-0Ts and ten 0-6-0Ts.

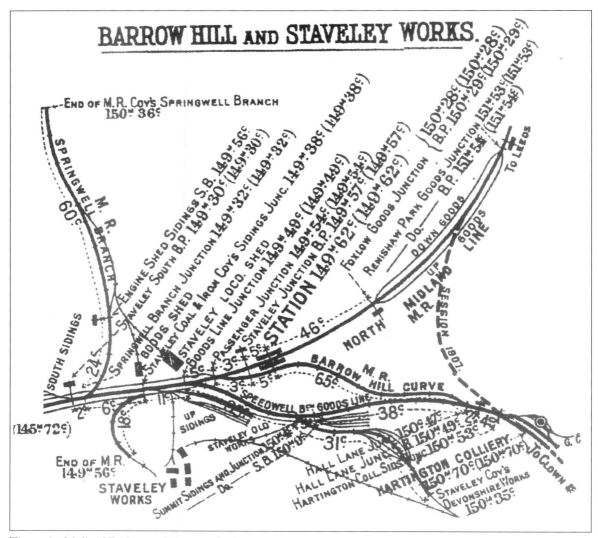

This is the Midland Railway mileage map for Barrow Hill and Staveley Works.

Introduced by the Midland Railway in 1907 these 0-4-0Ts with their short wheelbases were ideal for working in and around factories, breweries and docks. On 1 January 1948, three of the class were to be found at Staveley (Barrow Hill): Nos. 41528, 41529 and 41534. By August 1950 Nos. 41531, 41532, 41533 and 41534 were at Hasland. After a spell at Gloucester – July 1951 to September 1952 – No.41533 returned to Derbyshire and Staveley (Barrow) moving to the nearby former Great Central shed by August 1958. In January 1967 No.41533 along with sister engine No.41528; half-cabs No's.41708, 41734, 41763, 41804, 41835 and 0-4-0STs No's.47000 and 47001 were to be found in a siding at Rotherham Masboro' awaiting cutting up.

The Hawker Siddeley experimental locomotive *Kestrel* at Staveley on 15 September 1969 was not only the most powerful locomotive to run on British Railways, its Sulzer 16 LVA24 4,000 metric horsepower engine with six 515hp traction motors made it the most powerful single unit in the world. It ran 125,000 miles in service on BR before bring sold to the Soviet Union in 1971.

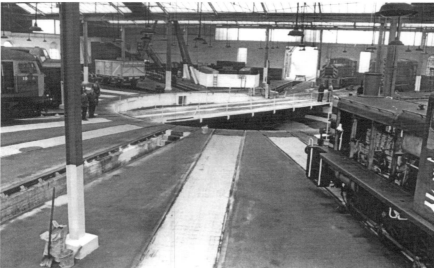

Barrow Hill roundhouse, the last operational roundhouse in the UK, in September 1970.

Though Staveley (Barrow Hill) closed to steam in October 1965, it remained in use as a stabling point for locomotives assigned to merry-go-round (MGR) trains until February 1991. It was then purchased by Chesterfield Borough Council for use as a working museum and is open to visitors most weekends. Our picture inside the roundhouse was taken during a BR open day.

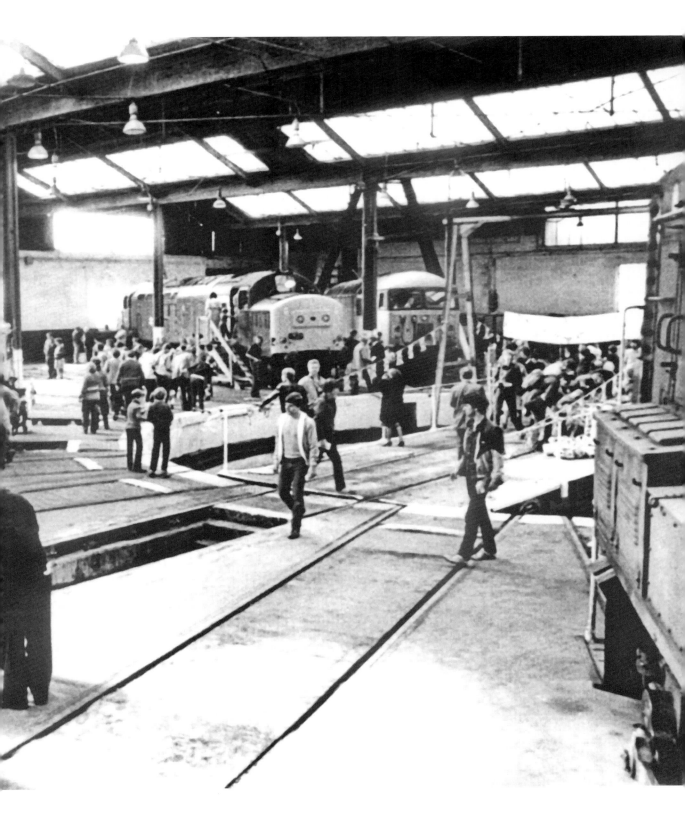

1Co-Co1 Class 45 No.45048 and a pair of Class 55 Deltics at Barrow Hill.

Hump shunting duties at Tinsley Yard, Sheffield, called for something more powerful than BR's standard 350hp 0-6-0 diesel-electric locomotives. The problem was solved by permanently coupling two 350s together to produce a 0-6-0+0-6-0 master and slave locomotive, one of which is seen here during a Barrow Hill open day. Three were completed at Darlington Works during 1965. D4500 was coupled to D4188; D4501 to D4190 and D4502 to D4187. As only one cab was needed, the slave units lost theirs. Under BR's reclassification they became Class 13, numbered 13001 to 13003. No.13002 was the first to go, being withdrawn in June 1981. The other two went in January 1985. When first completed, master and slave were coupled cab-to-cab. On 21 February 1967 BR's last 1hp unit was withdrawn from service. *Charlie*, a 17-hand, 24-year-old shunting horse retired from duty at Newmarket where he had spent much of his career shunting horseboxes.

These pictures are just two of a large series recording the construction of Staveley Works. By this date the contractor's wagons would not have been allowed out onto the main line as strict standards on construction, couplings, axles and brakes had been introduced by the Railway Clearing House in 1887. The locomotive also belonged to the contractor. (Chesterfield Local Studies Library)

Early 20th century view of Staveley Works. Note the rope-worked incline in the foreground. (Chesterfield Local Studies Library)

This picture of a busy time at Staveley's tarred slag plant is thought to date from the 1930s. (Chesterfield Local Studies Library)

The crew of Staveley Coal & Iron Co. 0-4-0ST *Sir William* pose for the camera in this picture thought to date from 1930, the year *Sir William* was delivered new from builders Andrew Barclay & Co. of Kilmarnock. Staveley also owned and operated several locomotives built at the Broad Oak Works of Markham & Co. of Chesterfield. These included the 0-4-0STs *Dunston* and *Staveley* (both built in 1890); *G. Bond (*built 1893*)*; *Gladys* (built 1894); *Lily* (built 1909), and the Ireland Colliery-based 0-6-0ST *Violet* (built 1895). (Chesterfield Local Studies Library)

Referring to the previous picture here is *Staveley*. (Vic Hall)

Ireland Colliery was part of the Staveley Coal & Iron Co. empire in Derbyshire, along with Bond's Main, Temple Normanton and Markham Collieries. The company also owned Warsop Main Colliery in Nottinghamshire, while Northamptonshire subsidiaries included the Cranford Ironstone Co., the Loddington Ironstone Co., and Burton Latimer Ironstone Pits. The Eastwell Ironstone Co. in Leicestershire and the Pilton Ironstone Co., Luffenham, Rutland, were also subsidiaries. Ireland was sunk in 1874; one of the new 'high-tech' deep mines of the  day was developed to replace the shallow pits in the area. For nearly 20 years the colliery had its own coke ovens but these became redundant on the commissioning of Staveley Works in 1907. In the left background is the LNER's Staveley engine shed. (Chesterfield Local Studies Library)

Like Clowne, Creswell village was also served by two stations; one on the Great Central line, the other on the Midland line to Mansfield. To avoid confusion, the Great Central Station was renamed Creswell & Welbeck in September 1897, while the Midland Station appeared in the timetables as

Elmton & Creswell from May 1886. Creswell & Welbeck closed to passengers on 10 September 1939 – a victim of wartime rationalisation – and closed completely on 28 November 1949. Elmton & Creswell closed to goods traffic on 6 January 1964 and to passengers during the following October, though private sidings remained in use a little while longer. Both of these pictures were originally published as postcards; the one above dates from the Great War, when women took over all manner of jobs due to large numbers of men being away with the armed forces.

Within a few years of services being withdrawn between Mansfield Woodhouse and Worksop via Whitwell, Creswell and Shirebrook, it became apparent that there were grounds for reopening the line to passenger traffic. This was due to the overall increase in population in the area, as well as the fact that more and more people were commuting to work. As Whitwell's Station had been dismantled and moved to Butterley, the village got a new one when the Robin Hood line reopened for passenger traffic. (Clive Hardy)

Pilsley station was situated at the highest point above sea level on the Great Central main line between London and Sheffield. It closed to all traffic on 2 November 1959.

This is a sorry looking Whitwell station on 4 February 1980: the picture is one of a series taken for a story announcing that the building was to be taken down stone-by-stone for eventual re-erection at the Midland Railway Centre, Butterley. Whitwell had closed to passenger traffic on 12 October 1964 and to goods traffic on 14 June 1965.

TO BUXTON VIA THE CROMFORD–HIGH PEAK

One of the Cromford &
High Peak line's ex-North
London Railway 0-6-0Ts is
seen here approaching
Cromford at some time in
1952. These powerful little
engines with their short
wheelbase were ideal for
working the C&HPR and
several were allocated to
Rowsley for that purpose by
the LMS. (C.M. & J.M.
Bentley)

Ex-North London Railway 0-6-0T No.58850 simmers gently at Cromford Wharf on 25 April 1953. The 73-year-old
veteran was a long way from home, having been built at Bow Works in 1880 as NLR No.76, though from 1891 until the
LNWR took over in 1909 she was No.116. Her last tour of duty on the C&HPR was at Middleton Top during 1959,
though by the September of that year she was stored there. Later stored at Rowsley, she was withdrawn from service in
March 1960 and taken to Derby Locomotive Works where she was overhauled and repainted as LNWR No.2650 prior
to going to the Bluebell Railway.

The modern era comes to Cromford Wharf in the guise of 204hp 0-6-0 diesel shunter No.D2380. The picture was taken by Harry Townley on 14 May 1965 and is the last image he ever took of the C&HPR. Sister locomotive D2383 took over from 0-4-0ST No.47000 on the Sheep Pasture Top–Middleton Bottom section in August 1966 and remained on the line until it closed in April 1967. (C.M. & J.M. Bentley)

One of the old C&HPR water tanks is preserved at the Ecclesbourne Railway, Wirksworth. It was pictured there on 15 August 2006. (Clive Hardy)

This picture was one of a number taken during an early 1950s visit to the Cromford & High Peak by the *Derbyshire Times*. A water tender and a wooden-bodied wagon are making the ascent at Sheep Pasture incline and have just passed the catch pit into which runaway descending vehicles could be diverted. The road is the main A6 and through the bridge another rake of wagons can be seen being prepared for the trip to the top.

The C&HPR was one of the more eccentric lines to be built. Derbyshire limestone was in demand; the roads were in no fit state to transport it, and the nearest canals were at Cromford or Whaley Bridge. Built to link the quarries with both canals, the 33-mile line passed through terrain that was wild and mountainous, leaving engineer Josias Jessop no alternative other than to incorporate rope-worked inclines into the route. There were five inclines on the climb from Cromford to the highest point on the line at Ladmanlow and four more on the descent to Whaley Bridge. By 1831 the line was up and running, though at this stage the level sections were worked with horses.

A rake of loaded stone wagons descends the 1,349-yard-long Sheep Pasture incline on a continuous wire rope 2,880 yards in length, the gradient varying between 1 in 8 and 1 in 9. The number of daily runs up and down the incline varied according to traffic. On 25 March 1961 there were 35 runs, comprising a total of 40 loaded wagons going down, and 9 loaded and 16 empties going up.

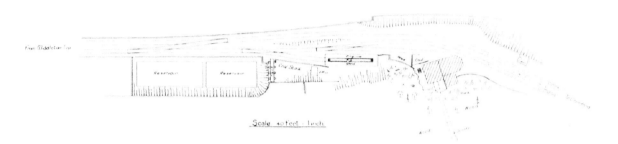

LMS track plan for Sheep Pasture Top. The shaded building is the Engine House for the incline.

The 18in (450mm) gauge Steeple Grange Light Railway operates over a stretch of the former trackbed of the Killers Quarry branch at Steeplehouse. The locomotive pictured here is ZM32, one of the smallest diesels to be owned by BR, built in 1957 by Ruston & Hornsby of Lincoln for use on the internal narrow gauge system at Horwich Locomotive Works. (Clive Hardy)

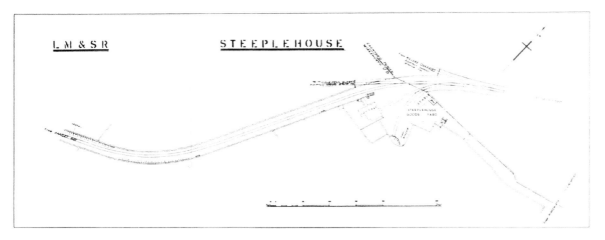

LMS track plan for Steeplehouse.

Middleton Top Engine House, restored by the Derbyshire Archaeological Society, houses a Butterley twin-cylinder 20hp low-pressure condensing beam engine dating from 1825. (Clive Hardy)

An echo of how it used to be at Middleton Top? This picture, taken on Friday 15 February 2008, shows an old wooden-bodied goods wagon painted in Midland Railway colours, perched on a short length of track at the top of the incline. The signal, which is in approximately the correct position, isn't the original: that was a rather handsome wooden-post lower quadrant. When the incline was in use the signal was lowered – hence lower quadrant – to indicate that a rake of two or three wagons or water tenders were ready to begin their descent. (Clive Hardy)

The last day of operation on the Cromford & High Peak – 30 April 1967 – and the last two J94s 0-6-0STs active on BR Nos.68012 and 68006, haul a Stephenson Locomotive Society special of brake vans over the line. The following month No.68006 was officially withdrawn; No.68012 lasted a few months longer, being transferred to Westhouses shed to work at Williamthorpe Colliery alongside 0-6-0T No.47289. When both were withdrawn on 14 October their respective classes became extinct on BR. (Clive Hardy)

Here we make a slight detour off the C&HPR to Hartington on the Parsley Hay–Ashbourne line where Buxton's Ivatt 2-6-0 No.46401 does the honours with a water tank on 29 March 1965. Though the station had officially closed to all traffic on 6 July 1964, the station yard still saw some action as the village's water supply had to be brought in by rail. The track bed now forms part of the Tissington Trail. (C.M. & J.M. Bentley)

Buxton's allocation of ex-LNWR 0-8-0s could be found performing a variety of duties ranging from working the Birkenhead freight, banking to Briggs Sidings or Bibbington, shunting, and trip working. They also worked over the Ashbourne line, and here No.49446 is pictured clanking through Hartington in 1962, though by the September of that year she would be stored on the Buxton shed cripple road with 0-8-0s Nos.49281, 49262, 49350 and 49465. One of this class survived into preservation and was restored to working order at Pete Waterman's LNWR workshops at Crewe. (C.M. & J.M. Bentley)

Back to the C&HPR and Friden on 1 September 1965 where Ivatt 2-6-0 No.46401 was to be found at work. The engine's last working prior to withdrawal was from Briggs Sidings to Buxton on 30 April 1966. (C.M. & J.M. Bentley)

Parsley Hay was the junction of the C&HPR and the LNWR line to Ashbourne and Uttoxeter. This picture looking towards Buxton was taken on 10 June 1962. (C.M. & J.M. Bentley)

Parsley Hay looking south on 10 June 1962. (C.M. & J.M. Bentley)

0-8-0 No.49277 engaged in a little light shunting at Parsley Hay on 26 October 1961. (C.M. & J.M. Bentley)

Buxton-based Fowler 4F 0-6-0 No.44315 on snowplough duties at Briggs Sidings on 6 February 1963. (C.M. & J.M. Bentley)

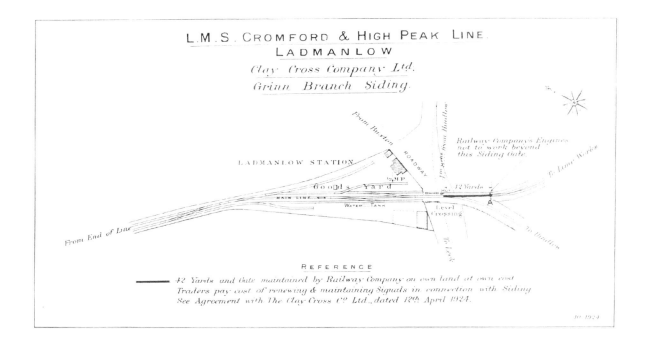

3F 0-6-0 No.43618 arrives at Ladmanlow with a joint Stephenson Locomotive Society/Manchester Locomotive Society special in April 1953. The tour had covered the whole of the C&HPR as well as the Wirksworth branch. At Friden the participants had clambered out of, or down from, the four open wagons and three brake vans that had so far been their method of conveyance and into three bogie coaches that would take them on to Ladmanlow. The motive power also changed. Having been hauled by the C&HPR's ageing ex-North London Railway 0-6-0Ts they were now going to jog along behind an ex-Midland 0-6-0.

Landmanlow had effectively become the western terminus of the C&HPR in June 1892 with the opening of the line from Hurdlow to Buxton; a much easier route that allowed the abandonment of Bunsall incline.

Class 60 No.60097 winds its way towards Buxton with a train from Hindlow on Monday 25 September 2006.

Stanier 4MT 2-6-4T No.42543 passes Higher Buxton with an 'Up' Uttoxeter in February 1953. Uttoxeter–Buxton passenger trains rarely comprised more than two coaches and as such were well within the capacity of these superheated two-cylinder tank engines. (C.M. & J.M.Bentley)

The 'Midland' side of Buxton station was closed to all traffic from 6 March 1967 with the withdrawal of passenger services to and from Millers Dale and on the Manchester–Derby main line. Little remains of this building today save for a section of wall from the gable end. The remainder was demolished and the site excavated out for the car park at the back of the Spring Gardens shopping centre.

Buxton Midland on 17 December 1963 with a diesel multiple unit on the Millers Dale service.

"Go by train to Derby for 10/-."

This picture of the former Midland station at Buxton was taken on 17 December 1963, when platforms 4 to 6 accommodated services over former Midland routes, while platforms in the old London & North Western part – the bit still in use – was for services via Dove Holes; Chapel-en-le-Frith South and Furness Vale to Manchester.

In 1980, Peak Rail acquired a site at Buxton where the old Midland station had once stood – pressing the former Midland goods shed, which was still standing, into use as a museum and shop. As the site was only five acres in area train operation was limited, but a line some 300 yards long was laid and, in 1984, the society began running passenger trains.

However, once the decision had been taken to concentrate efforts on reopening the Darley Dale–Matlock section, Buxton was in effect doomed. With neighbours Buxton Mineral Water keen to expand, the society did the sensible thing and sold up save for sufficient land on which to run trains when Buxton does eventually become the northern terminus of the line.

The locomotive feature here is 0-6-0ST *Brookes No.1* which was built by the Hunslet Engine Co of Leeds in 1941. It was from this design of engine that the wartime 'Austerity' 0-6-0ST was derived. (Baz Blood)

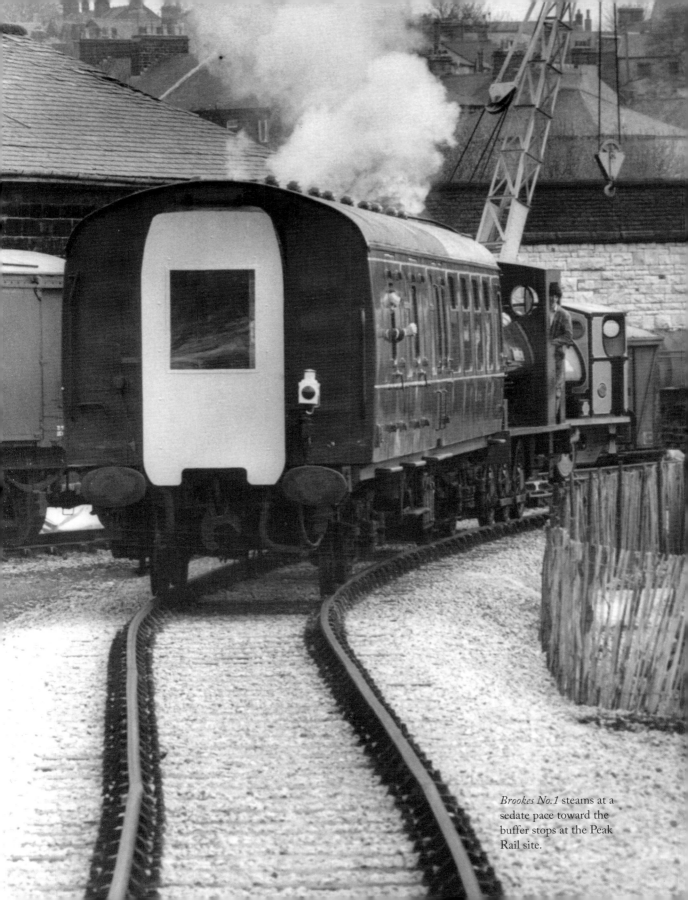

Brookes No.1 steams at a sedate pace toward the buffer stops at the Peak Rail site.

Another incumbent at the Peak Rail site was LMS 8F 2-8-0 No.48624 which had been rescued from a scrap yard at Barry. She is seen here in the early stages of restoration. (Baz Blood)

Heading for pastures new is 9F 2-10-0 heavy freight locomotive No.92214 – the first engine to be delivered to the Buxton site – is seen here in the process of being dismantled to allow its transportation to a new site following Peak Rail's decision to abandon Buxton for the time being. Completed in November 1959, like many of its classmates No.92214 had a relatively short working life on BR, being withdrawn and sold for scrap in September 1965. However, after languishing at Woodham's Scrapyard at Barry for a number of years she was eventually purchased for preservation. (Baz Blood)

"There may be trouble ahead..." Buxton's snow ploughs were usually to be found languishing in the Up Refuge Sidings, where trains to and from Great Rocks Junction are run round. However, a forecast of snow would soon see them lashed to a pair of Class 31 diesel-electrics and taken for a spin to Peak Forest and back to make sure all was in order. (Baz Blood)

Stanier Jubilee 4-6-0 No.45587 and Fowler 2-6-4Ts Nos.42306 and 42314 on Buxton shed in 1961. The number of 2-6-4Ts allocated to Buxton fell during the 1950s with the introduction of diesel multiple units, though Nos,42370 and 42371 remained the regular motive power on a couple of turns that continued to be steam hauled. For years No.42370 was the regular engine on the 08.00hrs Buxton–Manchester train, while No.42371's duties took it to foreign parts. Coming off shed, it would proceed light engine to Chinley, where it picked up four coaches and worked the 06.50hrs to Sheffield Midland. From there it worked the 07.50hrs to Rotherham Masborough followed by a return trip to Sheffield. It then hauled the 09.39hrs "all stations to Chinley" where it performed a bit of shunting prior to returning light to Buxton. No.42370 went to Crewe for breaking up in early 1961; the last 2-6-4T at Buxton (No.42379) left for Newton Heath in early July 1963. (C.M. & J.M.Bentley)

4F 0-6-0 No.44599 on Buxton shed on 7 November 1965. In 1911 the Midland introduced its new enlarged 0-6-0 goods engine design, eventually building 192 of them: Nos.3825–4026. The LMS continued construction, building another 575 of them between 1924 and 1940. All survived into nationalisation as Nos.44027–44606. The diagonal line painted on the yellow cab side was applied to all steam locomotives banned from running under the overhead electrification wires south of Crewe. (C.M. & J.M.Bentley)

11 March 1993 saw Class 37 No.37415 *Highland Region* on its first revenue-earning run – a trip to from Tunstead to Hindlow and back – since its transfer from Scotland. About half a dozen Scottish Class 37s were cascaded down to North West Freight. A couple of drivers on night turns were sent to pick them up from Longsight Traction Maintenance Depot, Manchester, bringing them to Buxton by way of Peak Forest and Great Rocks Junction.

Closer examination revealed that several of these engines were a little worse for wear. At least one of them had so many holes in its No.1 end cab sides at footplate level that when it was driven, a freezing gale blew round the cab. As a stop gap measure, it had to be paired up with another Class 37 so that it could only be driven from its No.2 end cab until repairs had been carried out.

One driver also related that when he went to take another pair out on a run he had difficulty shutting his cab door. Having run out of patience he got his weight behind the door and slammed it shut, whereupon some of the cab windows fell out! (Baz Blood)

When 1Co-Co1 Class 45 No.45034 was withdrawn from main line service in July 1987, it had already survived for longer than many of its classmates. That wasn't the end, however, as the locomotive was still in full working order, and during the following November it was transferred to Departmental Stock along with Class 45's Nos.45022, 45029, 45040 and 45066. All five were sent to Gateshead to work as Civil Engineering Department trains and were later allocated to Tinsley from where they were withdrawn for a second time. Nos. 97409 (45022) and 97411 (45034) went in July 1988; Nos.97410 (45029), 97412 (45040) and 97413 (45066) went the following month. (Baz Blood)

This BR/Brush Type 4Co-Co diesel-electric was built at Crewe in December 1965 as No.D1980 and sent new to Gateshead. In March 1974 it was renumbered 47278 under BR's TOPS scheme. (Baz Blood)

Since the closure of Buxton TMD, the Middle Road at the station is sometimes used for the stabling of engineering vehicles. Here, on 5 December 2004, a grubby looking Class 37 No.37706 on Sandite duty is parked up between turns. The Class 37 at the other end of the ensemble is No.37682. Also pictured at an earlier date is First Engineering's DR 73914.

This is Chapel-en-le-Frith on the former LNWR line to Manchester via Furness Vale. Both pictures were taken on 2 August 2000. The DMU No.150148 is pictured at 17.08hrs drawing into the station on its way to Manchester Piccadilly. The picture inside the signal box was taken at 17.41hrs: a busy time by Chapel standards with all signals cleared as there are trains in both directions.

Chapel-en-le-Frith

It would be impossible to take a look at railways around Buxton and not mention the events of 9 February 1957. Earlier that day Driver John Axon had experienced problems with steam escaping from the steam-brake handle of his Stanier 8F 2-8-0 No.48188 whilst working to Buxton with an unfitted freight from Warrington Arpley. At Buxton shed, it appeared that the problem had been cured when a fitter tightened up a loose nut, so with no cause for concern Axon backed his charge onto the return working in readiness to depart at 11.05hrs. His train comprised 33 wagons plus a brake van and together with the locomotive amounted to somewhere in the region of 775 tons. On departure, Axon's train would be banked in rear as far as Bibbington Sidings by another Stanier 8F 2-8-0.

However, shortly after setting off steam began escaping again. Axon attempted to deal with the problem, but as the train approached Bibbington Sidings distant signal, the union pipe blew apart releasing scalding steam into the cab. Though Axon and his fireman managed to screw down the tender handbrakes, it was impossible to get anywhere near the regulator or sound the alarm on the whistle. Axon, staying with the engine in the hope of regaining control, ordered Fireman Scanlon to bail out and drop as many wagon handbrakes as he could.

From the brake van, Guard Ball, on spotting Scanlon attempting to drop handbrakes, sensed trouble and did the only thing he could; he applied the brake in his van. Ball had been working with Axon all week and knew his driver always stopped at Bibbington Sidings, to pin down around half the wagon brakes. Pinning

down, done when a train is at a stand, secures a brake block against a wagon wheel; as opposed to dropping, which merely brings the block into contact with the wheel. On level going dropping might have helped but on a gradient it would have little effect.

At Dove Holes, Signalman Fox would soon face one of those impossible situations dreaded by all signallers. Some minutes earlier he had released a Rowsley–Edgeley freight out of the Down loop and this was now trundling down towards Chapel-en-le Frith at a sedate 15–20mph. Now he had Axon's freight almost on him, steam billowing from the cab and Axon leaning out frantically waving his arms. Fox interpreted this as Axon wanting the points set for main line. The signalman had only a couple of seconds to decide his course of action. He could put Axon into the loop and let him crash there, or he could run him main line in the hope that the driver would regain control. He chose the latter but immediately contacted Chapel box to let them know they had a runaway heading in their direction. Meanwhile at Chapel station the 10.20hrs two-car diesel multiple unit service from Manchester London Road was standing in the platform, unable to proceed towards Buxton due to a late-running freight in the section ahead.

In those days the signalbox was situated just beyond the Buxton direction platform, and the DMU guard had walked up to it to find out why his train was being delayed. Events quickly unfolded. On hearing of the runaway the guard ran back shouting a warning to his driver. Meanwhile a Buxton-based driver who was travelling on the DMU wised up to what was happening and immediately evacuated the passengers out of the train and clear of the station. The DMU driver who was already out of his cab when his guard shouted the warning had by now spotted not only the Rowsley freight but Axon's runaway closing fast behind it. Pointing back he shouted a warning to the Rowsley crew, but time had run out and Axon's train slammed into it destroying the brake van and the last three wagons and killing Guard Creamer. The tremendous impact derailed Axon's locomotive which fell onto its right hand side and ploughed into the platform. Its tender arced through the air and smashed through the signalbox. As wagons from Axon's train piled into a heap the shock wave derailed several wagons towards the front end of the Rowsley train.

John Axon could have jumped clear, but instead chose to remain with his locomotive and to attempt to regain control. His courage was recognised with the posthumous award of the George Cross and in 2007, a plaque commemorating the events of that day was unveiled at Chapel-en-le-Frith station.

On 5 June 1965, Wallace Oakes was in charge of a Euston–Carlisle express, when near Winsford, Cheshire, the cab became enveloped in flames caused by a blow-back from the firebox. Despite suffering severe burns Driver Oakes stayed at the controls and brought the train to a stand safeguarding the lives of his passengers and preventing a crash. He died of his injuries seven days later. On 19 February 1981, BR honoured both John Axon and Wallace Oakes, who had also received the George Cross. Electric locomotives Nos. 86260 and 86261 were named *Driver Wallace Oakes GC* and *Driver John Axon GC* respectively.

On the day of the incident at Chapel-en-le-Frith, the Derby Breakdown Crane with its lifting capacity of 45 tons was on the scene at a little after 16.00hrs. It can be seen here the following day tackling the tangled debris which in some places was 25 feet high. The Crewe Breakdown Crane arrived from the Stockport side of the crash by 17.00hrs at the latest, and by 17.30hrs emergency lighting had been rigged enabling a preliminary inspection to be carried out. (C.M. & J.M. Bentley)

Access to the site was restricted on 10 February to allow the bodies of Driver Axon and Guard Creamer to be recovered. Fire crews remained on hand to hose away the limestone dust which covered much of the station and the crash site. (C.M. & J.M. Bentley)

Having been re-railed, No.48188 stands in Chapel goods yard awaiting removal at walking pace to Buxton shed. There it would be prepared for its two-day journey to Derby Works for repairs. En-route it would be given a further examination at Rowsley shed. The signal is an upper quadrant quickly installed in place of the destroyed LNWR lower quadrant. Basic signalling was operational within a week thanks to the installation of a four-lever Midland pattern ground frame. This enabled both lines to have working distant and starter signals. (C.M. & J.M. Bentley)

WIRKSWORTH

As a cost-cutting exercise the Midland Railway introduced steam-powered railmotors on the branch but unfortunately the gradients proved a little too severe, forcing the company to rethink its options. The answer was this eccentric ensemble, comprising a Midland & Great Northern 4-4-0T and an original Pullman car dating from 1874.

Preserved Midland Railway 3 cylinder compound 4-4-0 No.1000 at Wirksworth. On 7 September 1961 No.1000 was used to haul several preserved locomotives from Derby Works to Wirksworth for filming by the BBC for the TV programme *Railway Roundabout*. The other locomotives were Midland Railway 4-2-2 No.118; London, Tilbury & Southend Railway 4-4-2T No.80 *Thundersley*; and Midland Railway 2-4-0 No.158A.

0-4-4T No.58077 provided the motive power for a combined Stephenson Locomotive Society/Manchester Locomotive Society tour of the Wirksworth branch on 23 April 1953. Society members had already paid a visit to the Cromford & High Peak line and had journeyed to Wirksworth for lunch at the Red Lion prior to taking a round trip to Duffield behind No. 58077.

As the branch loop had already been lifted, No.58077 had to run round its train on the main line prior to returning to Wirksworth at 14.15hrs. Members then continued their journey to Buxton via the Cromford & High Peak. The trip was such an outstanding success that it was repeated a couple of months later.

These views of Wirksworth station yard are looking toward Cemetery Lane Bridge; the two-road engine shed can be seen in the distance. The line to Bowne & Shaw's quarry passes under the extreme right hand arch of the bridge. (C.M & J.M. Bentley)

British Rail often used the Wirksworth branch for running in locomotives fresh out of Derby Works, and as the setting for publicity photographs.

In 1923, the Midland was absorbed into the London, Midland & Scottish Railway. George Hughes, of the former Lancashire & Yorkshire Railway, was appointed Chief Mechanical Engineer of the new company, and the Midland's Sir Henry Fowler was made his assistant. In 1925 Hughes was succeeded by Sir Henry, and it was during his watch that the LMS acquired a new breed of 4-6-0 express passenger engines, as well as the massive 2-6-0+0-6-2 Beyer-Garratt freight locos for working heavy coal trains between Toton and Brentwood. In 1931 Sir Henry was succeeded by H.J. Lemon, who was only in the chair long enough to oversee the design of a class of 0-4-4Ts before being promoted to Vice-President Traffic and Operations. His replacement was Swindon Works trained William Stanier.

Stanier was brought in because he would not be influenced by the small engine policy of the old Midland Railway, and was likely to come up with designs for more powerful locomotives. When loadings had demanded it, the Midland had always chosen to use two small engines instead of one large one. For reasons best known to himself, Stanier took an instant dislike to several preserved engines at Derby Works and ordered them to be cut up.

One such engine was LMS No.1, which had recently been restored and repainted in Midland Railway livery carrying her old duplicate number 156A. Designed by Matthew Kirtley, 29 of these 2-4-0 passenger engines were built in the 1860s, forming the Midland's 156 Class. They were subsequently rebuilt and 22 survived long enough to pass into LMS ownership carrying Nos. 1–22.

Meanwhile LMS No.20002, the engine formerly known as No.2, was still hard at work and happily avoided Stanier's attention. The old engine served throughout the Second World War, and survived to be taken into British Railway's ownership. In 1948, at the grand old age of 82, she was restored to Midland Railway livery as No.158A and is seen here during filming for BBC TV's *Railway Roundabout*.

In 1974 BR began to refurbish its diesel multiple unit fleet. This is the first three-car unit to be put through the programme and is pictured here on the Wirksworth branch for a publicity shoot. The livery is off-white with a blue waistband. It later put in publicity appearances at Sheffield Midland and Manchester Piccadilly. The local press in both cities running stories to the effect that it was the first unit to be refurbished for their respective Passenger Transport Executives but all BR did was change the PTE logo prior to each visit.

This Ultra Light Rail Vehicle was recently returned to Wirksworth in August 2006, after being on exhibition at the National Railway Museum at York. Wyvern Rail offers training facilities at Wirksworth for private companies as well as location filming for TV.

In 2008 the railway won a role in developmental work being carried out by Thales Rail Signalling Solutions for the new transmission-based train control system (TBTC). Train and track-based sensors detect the location of a train, the theory being that such a system will allow increased line capacity as safety clearances can be reduced. A control centre has been established by Wash Green Bridge and a modified battery-electric locomotive is to be used on an 18-month test programme. If successful the system will be rolled out on London Underground's Jubilee, Northern and Piccadilly lines in time for the 2012 Olympics.

For nigh on 30 years, observant railway enthusiasts driving south-bound across the Ml Tinsley Viaduct at Sheffield, would have seen a couple of saddle tanks lurking in the yard of a nearby road haulage depot. In October 2005 the engines, both built by Andrew Barclay & Co. of Kilmarnock, arrived at the Wirksworth headquarters of the Ecclesbourne Railway for assessment as to their possible return to steam. Tuesday 15 August 2006 found old No.3 (Andrew Barclay 2360 of 1954) moved from its storage site to a more convenient location where it could be worked on. Though not considered powerful enough, and probably lacking sufficient coal capacity to haul Ecclesbourne's proposed services to and from Duffield, these saddle tanks are ideal hauling brake van rides along the old quarry branch.

The visitors might have gone but that does not mean the work stops – far from it! Keeping a railway operational involves a great deal of behind the scenes work. Here, one of Ecclebourne's diesel shunters propels a couple of ballast wagons out of the siding prior to heading off in the opposite direction along the main running line to where a track gang was hard at work.

In 1966, Middlepeak Quarry, Wirksworth took delivery of its first diesel locomotive which had been purchased second hand from Ind Coope at Burton-upon-Trent. Its arrival allowed the quarry to relegate one of its steam engines, 0-4-0ST *Holwell No.3*, a venerable machine dating from 1873, to standby duties.

In June 1970 the arrival of a second diesel resulted in 0-4-0ST *Uppingham* being taken out of service. No longer needed, the steam engines were dumped outside at the back of the

shed: *Holwell No.3* was sheeted over; *Uppingham* was left to face the elements. During the spring of 1972 both diesels failed and *Uppingham* was returned to steam though in the mean time its chimney cap had rusted through and fallen off.

AROUND THE
MIDLAND RAILWAY CENTRE

The first Midland Railway Centre public passenger-carrying train departs from Butterley for Swanwick Junction on 22 August 1981, just four days after Derbyshire County Council had transferred the trackbed lease to the society. Following visits from the Railways Inspectorate, the condition of the line was deemed suitable enough for a Light Railway Order to be signed on 25 July and BR transferred ownership of the trackbed to Derbyshire County Council. 0-6-0T No.16440, built in 1926 by the North British Locomotive Co., was used on the first services, with each train consisting of four coaches.

Designed by Henry Fowler, no less than 422 of these versatile engines were built for the LMS between 1924 and 1931. Though primarily intended for shunting, they were equally at home on trip working and local passenger duties. Eleven have survived into preservation, four of which are at the Midland Railway Centre: Nos.47327, 16440 (BR No.47357), 47445 and 47564.

On Monday 25 September 2006, the preserved 0-6-0T No.47327 is in light steam at Swanwick Junction for the first time since undergoing an overhaul. Volunteers were applying the finishing touches necessary to transform the 80-year-old locomotive into *Thomas the Tank Engine*.

Forty years had passed since BR Standard Class 9 2-10-0 No.92219's withdrawal from service when this picture was taken on 25 September 2006, but it looks as though many more will pass before this giant of steam is restored to working order. Along with Nos 92218 and 92220, she was one of the last three steam locomotives to be constructed for BR, and was completed at Swindon Works in January 1960.

A casualty of the 1960s policy to 'modernise' BR, No.92219 was withdrawn from service in August 1965 when in railway terms she was hardly run in let alone worn out. Along with a couple of hundred other engines she finished up at Woodharn's Scrapyard, Barry, from where she was eventually rescued in May 1988.

The first of 172 BR Standard 5MT 4-6-0 No.73000 was completed at Derby Works in April 1951; the last No.73171 being turned out by Doncaster in May 1957. Derby was responsible for the construction of 125 of the class and one of them, No.73154, held the distinction of being the last steam locomotive built at the Works.

Thirty of the class Nos 73125–73154 were fitted with the Caprotti valve gear, which allowed excellent steam distribution due to the cylinder inlet valves being driven by cams worked by rotating shafts. These were connected to the return crank axlebox, itself linked to the driving wheel crank pin. As with the Giesel Oblong Ejector, which was fitted to 2-10-0 No.92250 in 1958 to lower coal consumption, The Caprotti valve gear was one of BR's last attempts at improving steam locomotive performance.

No.73129 was withdrawn in November 1967 and rescued from Woodham's Scrapyard, Barry, in 1973. In working order when this picture was taken, it is the sole survivor of the 30 fitted with the Caprotti valve gear.

1Co-Co1 diesel-electrics D1–D10 were built at Derby Works during 1959–60 and each was named after a British mountain. By 1980 there were three survivors; Nos.44004 *Great Gable*, 44007 *Ingleborough*, and 44008 *Penyghent*, all of which were allocated to Toton. *Great Gable* is seen here after being repainted at Toton in August 1980 in near-original livery: Brunswick green body, mid-grey roof, silver-grey stripe and grilles. Her last revenue earning run was the 11.35hrs Toton–Rugby coal train on 28 November 1980.

Manchester–Wath EM2 Co-Co electric 27000 in the exhibition hall at the Midland Railway Centre, Swanwick Junction, on 25 September 2006.

This horsebox was built by BR in 1948 to an LMS design. It was derived from an even earlier Midland Railway one dating back to 1904. When the vehicle, which is 21ft long, 8ft 6ins wide, and weighs in at ten tons was being restored, it was found that BR had used recycled fittings from scrapped vehicles. Once a common sight on the railway network, the last horseboxes were withdrawn from service in 1968. As well as room for the horses these boxes were fitted with an accommodation compartment for a groom. However, grooms travelling in these vehicles were classed as goods and not passengers.

No.46203 *Princess Margaret Rose* was the first of ten production run Princess Royal Class express passenger engines built for the LMS. Designed by William Stanier to meet a requirement for a locomotive capable of hauling the Euston–Glasgow expresses which weighed in at over 500 tons, No.6203 entered traffic on 1 July 1935 having cost £8,538 to build. Her high capacity tender, capable of holding 4000 gallons of water and 9 tons of coal, cost an additional £1,154.

Withdrawn from BR stock on 20 October 1962, the engine was scheduled for scrapping, but thankfully Billy Butlin stepped in and bought it for display at his holiday camp at Pwllheli. The fact that several other locomotives survived the cutter's torch is solely due to Butlin buying them for display purposes. Repainted in LMS livery, the engine remained a visitor attraction at Pwhelli until 10 May 1975 when an agreement between Butlins and the Midland Railway Company saw her moved to Derby and eventually to Butterley.

In October 1988 *Princess Margaret Rose* was sold to Brell Ewart, who set about restoring it to running order and on 8 May 1990 a fire was lit in the firebox for the first time in nearly 30 years. Running in trials followed, and on 17 May the engine hauled a loaded test train from Derby to Sheffield and back to Derby. On 2 June it hauled the Richard Levick

Memorial train on two round Derby–Sheffield–Derby trips, and on 15 September No.46203 was in charge of *The White Rose*, again a Derby–Sheffield–Derby run. The year rounded off with a change of scenery, when on 10 November it hauled *The Red Rose* a trip from Nottingham to Didcot and back. The following year, *Princess Margaret Rose* put in appearances on a number of named tours including the Cambrian Mountain Express; The Midlander; The Westmorelander, and The Ynys-Mon Express.

This is the original Butterley station, pictured here on a postcard published before the Great War. The station closed to passengers in June 1947 and to goods traffic in November 1964, after which the buildings were demolished. When the Midland Railway Trust took over the site they were able to restore the station to its former glory, and the old Whitwell station building was available. This was taken down brick by brick, brought to Butterley and re-erected.

The former Whitwell station building re-erected at Butterley and restored to its 1875 appearance.